Journeyman

(A craftsman who has served his time)

Walter Partridge

Jan 1992

'The Printer's Chapel' *Wood Engraving* *Howard Phipps 1991*

JOURNEYMAN

A printer's impressions through eighty years
in a rapidly changing world

BY
WALTER PARTRIDGE

PERDIX PRESS
1991

Perdix Press is the Private Press of the author.
The front cover photograph is by Mike Newnez.
The frontispiece wood engraving of the Perdix pressroom is by Howard Phipps.

First published by Perdix Press
21 The Close, Salisbury, SP1 2EB.

Printed in Great Britain by
Antony Rowe Ltd., Chippenham, Wiltshire.

ISBN 0 907596 19 3

CONTENTS

Recovering memories, selecting some, rejecting others, making up the principles of inclusion or exclusion in a largely ad hoc way, being led on trails you never expected by the insistence of memories you never expected – the whole business sometimes seems a sort of confection or concoction, a construction made from old rope and orange boxes at the back of your mental garret.

Richard Hoggart, *A Sort of Clowning, Life and Times 1940–1959*

Foreword

by Leslie Thomas

WALTER PARTRIDGE is not an old friend. I met him one Saturday morning only a few weeks ago and that afternoon he came to try to teach me how to fish with a dry fly in the Wiltshire Avon at the bottom of my garden.

He told me that he was just before his eightieth birthday. He *had* to tell me because I, for one of many, would not have believed it. This spare, thoughtful, wryly humorous man with a toothy grin, is a walking – no striding – advertisement for life itself; he gives hope to those of us who are approaching old age with doubt and diffidence.

This endearing book is about his good life. His grandfather, a Norfolk farm worker, was ejected (with wife and thirteen children) from his cottage because he would not tell his employer how he intended to vote in an election and, vastly adding to the sin, had become a Methodist! The local vicar acted as bailiff. The family borrowed a horse and cart and drove to Hull to start again.

You can imagine Walter Partridge making the same stand as his grandfather. The East Anglian accent has been lost to a measured Yorkshire voice. He is, from this book and from our short acquaintanceship, someone without pretence or pretension. Twice in his life, first as a printer and then as an army officer, he was reprimanded for being too friendly and familiar with underlings.

There is much to enjoy in his story. But the descriptions of his craft, of the machines and men of this printing trade, and the technicalities, the wonderful words of the trade, are even better than the rest of this wholly enjoyable book.

Walter Partridge is a human, humane and humorous man. My only regret is that we did not meet long ago.

Leslie Thomas
Salisbury, Wilts.
August 1991

Preface

TO THIS BRIEF autobiographical account of more than sixty years in printing and publishing I have added a few paragraphs of social history from the late nineteenth century when my grandparents lived a hard life as farm workers in Norfolk, and included some of my own experiences with the Eighth Army in North Africa, Italy and Austria.

I have also introduced short profiles of the poet, R.C. Scriven, the artist, Jacob Kramer, the psychiatrist, Dr. Robert Ollendorf, and a number of the colourful characters who made Fleet Street such a fascinating human zoo when I worked there in the 'sixties and 'seventies.

I have included an account and bibliography of my retirement occupation with Perdix Press. It is my intention that this will be the final publication over the Perdix imprint, but you never can tell; I have retired several times before.

This book has been computer set and offset-printed. I would like to thank Sara and Keith Musgrove for their invaluable help in preparing this material for the press, Antony Rowe for putting it into print, and my wife Betty for her loyal and devoted work as acting, unpaid proof-reader.

I hope that in bringing together these disparate impressions of a printer over a long life in the trade I have been able to produce an interesting account of one journeyman's journey.

W.J.P.
1991

1

Motivation
'Arrogance and Sensitivity'

I LIKE PEOPLE, all sorts of people: painters, parsons, poets, plumbers; even people other people may find it difficult to get on with: bank managers, tramps, eccentrics and American tourists, of whom there are plenty where I now live, here in Salisbury Cathedral Close. I chat to them about the Cathedral and its history and have made many lasting friendships.

I used to think that my favourite choice of occupation would be to have acted as a guide or courier for the British Council, taking diplomats for a day off around the Yorkshire Dales or the Lake District. I have no idea if such an appointment ever existed but the notion appealed to me. The nearest I came to it was as liaison officer with the Eighth Army in Italy, when I sometimes had to escort and guide senior officers from Allied Force Headquarters in Caserta who wanted to see a battle and hear the guns go off. On one such occasion, I had taken a general to some high ground which overlooked one of the many river crossings east of the Appenines, where units of the Fourth Indian Division were the advance troops. A squadron of American bombers was to have pattern-bombed the far bank to destroy German communications, but the load was dropped on the near side by mistake, with devastating results. Troops from our Fourth Indian Division suffered appalling casualties from what is now being described as 'friendly fire'.

I was not all that ambitious by nature; when the heat got uncomfortable I tended to get out of the kitchen. But there was some element of a driving force tucked away in my bones. When I was a very new printing apprentice in Knaresborough, I remember seeing the Master Printers' Journal on my boss's desk, and saying to myself: 'I'll be in that lot one day, just you see.' In 1974, I was Vice-Chairman of the British Federation of Master Printers' Economic Development Committee: not a world-shattering rise to fame, but a modest degree of progress. As Stephen Fry of *The Independent* wrote about a very different level of businessman, 'Hanson has that mixture of arrogance and sensitivity that characterises Yorkshiremen.'

In these early stages of my journey, I was alternately shy and bold, a bit like a salmon going up stream to spawn, first hiding in the deep pools and shadows and then boldly leaping the mill weir that stands in the way. I was probably one of the few village-apprenticed compositors to go through the Royal Military Academy at Sandhurst (a fellow cadet was returned to his unit for spreading marmalade on his slice of bread at breakfast) and be commissioned into the Inns of Court Regiment where, I have to confess, I didn't last long. 'Too familiar with the troops' was my squadron leader's comment as I recollect. Never mind. It's the journey that matters, not the arriving.

A chance meeting in Leeds with a man called David Holt, who was soon to join *The Observer* as Assistant

Manager, led to our travelling on the same train from Leeds to London. We spent two hours talking about newspapers, books and trades unions. When I got home, I said to my wife, Betty: 'I'll be on the staff of *The Observer* within a month, just you see.' And I was. I joined *The Observer* as Contract Manager in 1959. The 'contract' I was to manage was between *The Observer*, essentially a company of journalists with no printing plant of their own, and Times Newspapers at Blackfriars who printed *The Observer* every week.

That encounter on the train, which precipitated my move to Fleet Street, came after a situation where I had been helping R.C. Scriven, a northern poet, to get a volume of his poems published by Secker and Warburg. In 1959, Scriven had the idea of writing a three-decker novel based on the lives of my grandparents, the Mears of East Dereham, and his own family, the Scrivens, who were in the engineering business in Yorkshire. Seckers said they would publish the poems if Scriven would complete the novel. Some hopes! He was, by this time, totally blind and almost completely deaf.

Seckers did in fact publish Scriven's poems under the title, *The Year of the Phoenix and other poems* in 1969 in association with Partridge Printers, my own firm in Leeds, but only after I had agreed to do the printing without charge! Most of the fifty-nine poems had been published before in *Punch* and *The Tablet*.

The idea of the three-decker novel was to take the Mears story from my grandparents' days as farm labourers in Norfolk through to their emigration to Yorkshire. The brightest of their thirteen children, a handsome, auburn-haired daughter, first worked for and later married into a wealthy Yorkshire county family, the

Scrivens. The young couple left farming and went into an iron foundry business making wheels and rails for railway pioneers. Fortunes were made and succeeding Scrivens came to control a great steel empire. The industrialised second generation spread their investments into America during the First World War and lost everything in the 1929 Wall Street crash.

The eldest son of the third generation, still working in Yorkshire steel but no longer rich, joined the Royal Tank Regiment in 1940. He showed brilliant promise at Sandhurst and was killed leading a squadron of crusader tanks in the battle of El Alamein.

Briefly, these facts were going to be the basis on which a novel called *The Iron Horse* would be created. Scriven wrote the first 75,000 words which were rejected by Seckers, Putnam's and other publishers. Putnam's sent a very civil note in which they commented that the book was not really suitable for their list; it contained some charming and perceptive background material in period style, but the narrative and dialogue were weak. This last criticism was somewhat ironic given the fact that due to his deafness, it had been several years since Scriven had heard a dialogue of any sort.

The novel was never published; it died with Scriven in 1985. It was then that I decided to pick up the Mears–Partridge story and write an account of what happened to my forebears and myself over the last hundred years, beginning in the late nineteenth century and leading on to the last decade of this one.

But first let me tell you more about the poet who prompted the idea – R.C. Scriven.

* * *

When we left 70 Frenchgate, our wartime home in

Richmond where our daughters Judith and Ruth were born, we moved to an L-shaped grey stone house in Thorner, which lies between Leeds and Wetherby. It was a cold house in a village where we never felt like settling. Over the back wall, at Number One Virginia Terrace, lived the poet and playwright, R.C. Scriven, with his tall, handsome wife, Phyl, and their son, Marc, who slept on a couch in the kitchen. It was an end cottage with an outside lavatory that wouldn't flush, cracked windows, an ill-fitting door and a stone-flagged floor. Phyl had been a model. She had managed fashion shows for Louis Cope, Couturier, in Harrogate, when that northern spa was more fashionable.

Ronald Charles Scriven, locally known as Ratz, had been a journalist on the now defunct *Yorkshire Observer*. He had had verses published in *Punch* for twenty years until Malcolm Muggeridge became its editor and required a degree of political sophistication that Scriven could not provide. He freelanced for *The Yorkshire Post* and *The Tablet* and established a reputation as a radio dramatist with a series of plays, notably, *The Single Taper*, an intensely moving account of his own eye operation, performed, without anaesthetic, by Professor Black at Leeds General Infirmary.

Soon after Scriven married Phyl, he lost his job when the *Yorkshire Observer* closed down and she became too crippled with arthritis to carry on her work. Life was very hard on them. Scriven continued to write a daily piece of poetry for *The Yorkshire Post* which he dictated straight off the top of his head from a call box to the copy takers, basing the poem on some item from the morning's radio news. He also continued to write children's plays and verses for both radio and publishers.

Some of the BBC people at Leeds did their best to

avoid his calls and the high-pitched squeaky voice which so often 'phoned to blast them to hell for not accepting his indecipherable manuscripts.

Scriven was a squat, Chestertonian figure with a well-shaped rosy face that looked as if it had just been scrubbed with carbolic soap. He was as tidy as Phyl could make him but was still covered from chin to navel with snuff and gravy. When his sight had nearly gone, I took him to Wakefield Art Gallery to review an exhibition of paintings. He knew in detail all the older canvasses and the work of the younger painters. The pictures were leaning against the wall waiting to be hung. In order to read the names and titles, and get a closer look at the painting technique, Ratz lay prone on the floor and rolled from one canvas to another like a barrel off a brewer's dray, while Westwood, the gallery director, gazed in wonder at the sockless, unwashed ankles protruding from frayed trouser cuffs.

When one of Ratz's plays was being rehearsed at Broadcasting House in London, he and Phyl were invited to dine at the Savoy with the producer and other celebrities. They stayed with the author-journalist, Jane Gaskell, near Olympia, and I took them to Moss Bros. in Covent Garden to get kitted out for the occasion. With superb courtesy and not an atom of condescension, the morning-coated assistants took Ratz one way and Phyl the other and brought them back within half an hour looking like a duke and duchess; he in white tie and tails, she in floor-sweeping gold lamé. I was handed two Moss Bros. cartons containing their old clothes to carry out to the taxi.

Ronald Faux wrote in *The Times* on October 1st, 1971: 'Ronald Scriven is a Yorkshire poet with an eerily acute eye for colour and detail. The countryside of his verse has the sound and richness of reality. The sense of a man who loves the freshness of moors and summer pools and delights at the deepening tones of twilight spills from his poetry. He is totally blind and almost completely deaf. Facing these two great handicaps, he has earned a living through a lively output of verse reflecting the humour of the North, vividly describing the countryside and sights he has not seen for thirty years, in books of verse, radio plays in verse and poems for *Punch* and *The Yorkshire Post*.'

Scriven had several eye operations. One, on his left eye, involved cutting away a section of the pupil while he was conscious but under local anaesthetic. He describes it chillingly in *A Single Taper*, one of his early and greatly acclaimed verse plays for radio. It was favourably reviewed in The Lancet.

'Numbed by the kind cocaine
My eyeball aches and wearies of the white
Minute, three-quarter halo of hot gold wire
　Naked in the electric bulb …
Pale-fire
　Paled by the cocaine-film's colourless
　　drugged rain.

　It is not fair,
O, God, it is not fair
　That I, for whom shape, colour and form
Mean life
　Should have my eye cut into by a knife
And have to watch it happen.'

One of Scriven's most remarkable qualities was an

ability to draw instantly from a wealth of fact and quotations stored in his head.

'I cannot use a notebook or refer to books,' he would say. 'I have to use my memory. I can give you Milton and Shakespeare by the yard, *The Golden Treasury* I took in through my pores.'

His ability to take bare fact and build rich poetry from it was as active as ever. He constructed an impression in verse of York Minster which was produced on the BBC's Third Programme. A friend read to him the raw material from reference books and the verse rolled off the type-writer.

He wrote for years under the soubriquet 'Ratz' by which he was well-known until his death in 1985. He began contributing to *Punch* in 1935.

In his later life, Scriven drew heavily on boyhood experience and the recollections and pictures that burned in his memory. The trilogy about his boyhood was broad-cast and other verse plays based on his early years were commissioned. G.K. Chesterton said he lived for the rest of his life on ideas he had before he was twenty. Scriven told me he was having the same experience.

When Scriven was struggling to earn a guinea or two from book reviews, Phyl would read the books, comment on them and read aloud selected passages; he would then write the review. Phyl became exhausted, trying to cope with her own illness as well as her very demanding husband, and when she became unable to continue, I was asked to take over.

'You don't need to drink a whole barrel of beer to know if it's good or bad,' Scriven would say. 'Read me the intro and the chapter headings; now read me pages 1 to 4 and pages 100 and 200. Never give this cursory treatment to a writer's first book or the second. The first book must be read right through to see what it's made of: is it all good, all bad, or good in parts? How much promise does it show? Can the faults be remedied? And the second book must also be read even more thoroughly to see if the first was a flash in the pan or if experience is producing improvements in style or technique.'

Under Scriven's guidance, I started to do the reviews myself. I always read the books thoroughly, often twice. Then I would write him long letters about them in the style of reviews.

'Never show off,' he cautioned me. 'Never use an author's work as a platform to exhibit your own knowledge. At our level of reviewing that is covering a wide cross-section of subjects, the reviewer must give as objective an appraisal as possible to help the potential book buyer taste the contents. He must also produce a small, rounded-off essay which is interesting to read for the many who enjoy reading reviews but seldom buy or borrow books.'

After a good deal of practice, I eventually found my reviews appearing in *The Yorkshire Post* without a word altered, except, of course, the signature. This pleased me enormously. I often wonder if Bill Oliver, the Deputy Editor, knew that Scriven's reviews were being ghosted by an amateur? Even if he had found out, he was far too kind-hearted to have said or done anything about it. Among the titles I reviewed were: *The Bishop's Bonfire* by Sean O'Casey; *Joyce Carey: A Preface to his Novels* by Andrew Wright; *A Pearl to India* by Vincent Cronin; *Don't Type in Bed* by Peggy Warner; *The Red Priest* by Wyndham Lewis, and other books usually about topography or travel.

When we moved to London in 1960, the reviewing had to stop and my correspondence with Scriven dwindled to occasional letters. I once received four pages from him, obviously typed without a ribbon in the typewriter, since they were blank, with holes punched through where full stops should have been. He had folded the sheets, sealed them up in an envelope and had Phyl address it to me. It was quite a feat of diplomacy to think of an adequate reply to send him, since I had been unable to read a word of his intended letter. A typical Scriven letter reads:

'March 6, 1974

My dear Walter,

So much water, so many eels and God knows what quantities of what John Burns used to call liquid history have flowed under the Thames bridges since we were last in touch that I don't know where to begin in re-establishing our 1s. of c. First, I was so delighted to hear from you again. Secondly, it was Sinclair Lewis not Oscar who advised the literary aspirant to apply the seat of the pants to the seat of the chair. Thirdly, triumph. The BBC is in the autumn to publish in one volume 'Remembrance Falls from Heaven' the four first scripts of my childhood autobio, plus 'The Seasons of the Blind'. With intro. by Charles Lefeaux.

Penguin Education published last October 'The Thingummyjig' and 'The Poltergoose'. Each price 20p. Illustrated. Francesca Greenoak (lovely name) the editor, was rapturous.

I narrowly escaped having my right eye, the one that tells black from grey, taken out, simply because the ambulance drivers' strike prevented my trip to St. James for that distasteful operation. In the interim, my other eye, still useless as an eye, has recovered its health and strength and stopped hurting me.

Time: a quarter to three pip emma and I am now going out to test a mad rumour that the ale at the Fox is not what it used to be.

Write back, my dear Walter, and give me some news.

Love to you, Betty and the covey,

Charles.'

Apart from being blind, Scriven could only hear about ten per cent of what was spoken even directly into his snuff-laden, National Health deaf aid which usually had flat batteries and shrieked like an angry parrot if you got too close. He asked me to go with him as his eyes and ears to discuss his writings with Secker's representative, David Holt, at the Queen's Hotel in Leeds. As mentioned earlier, I travelled back to London with Holt.

Next day, I was asked to lunch with *The Observer* manager, Tristan Jones, who offered me a job as their Contract Manager at £3000 a year, a good salary in 1959. The offer didn't need much thinking about: my decision to move into an entirely new career in Fleet Street newspaper production was instantaneous. I remained chairman of my Leeds printing firm, appointing Haydn Scott as Managing Director to run the business, which he did with great energy and skill, while I set about the enjoyable and often frightening task of being the link man between *The Observer*, with its brilliant editorial staff, and its printers, Times Newspapers at Printing House Square.

2

THE MOVE TO FLEET STREET: *THE OBSERVER* AND THE *FINANCIAL TIMES*

THE SHORT WALK from Temple Station to Tudor Street took me through the Middle Temple, past the fountain and the beautiful, round Temple Church; through the quiet squares where black-robed barristers strode to and from chambers where men's fates were being determined or their innocence established; past the *News Chronicle* end of rowdy Bouverie Street, home of the *News of the World* and Northcliffe House, and of the *Daily Mail* works. Pressmen taking a break, surplus packers and dispatch men loafed about the pavements in gossiping groups, like anarchists plotting a revolution, which they probably were. A few yards further on, I could hear musicians and singers from the Guildhall School practising their scales and arpeggios, filling the air between the Embankment and Tudor Street with much more pleasant sounds than the scream of newspaper rotary presses.

From a quiet back street works in Leeds to this hub of the newspaper world had been quite a step.

I didn't move my family south until I had tried out the new situation for six months. First, I lived in lodgings in a goulash-flavoured block of flats in Swiss Cottage mainly occupied by Austro-Hungarian refugees. Then in 1960, we found a house on the Middlesex bank of the Thames just below Teddington Lock, with a garden running down to the river, and we left Leeds for good.

Our two daughters, Judith and Ruth, were away at college and the two boys, Nick and Jim, born in Leeds just after the war, were still at school. The boys found the move hard to take, leaving all their friends and finding their feet in a strange environment was difficult for them. Nick protested bitterly about his new school and Jim often refused to go without being dragged. He developed an Olympic standard of truancy, dividing his off days between Heathrow Airport and the cinemas in Richmond and Twickenham, according to how far he could spin out his train fare money. We tried not to lean on them too hard. Nick moved to a small grammar school, and eventually, Jim settled down at the local secondary school where he took a string of 'O' and 'A' levels.

Running my own business was not something that I had really enjoyed. I gained in experience and was able to give my family a better position than we might otherwise have had, but when the door opened into the wider world of national newspapers, I made sure that it didn't shut until I was on the inside.

I was warmed by the friendship of many well-known *Observer* journalists who saw in me a useful ally in their strivings to get bigger and better papers out of *The Times* pressroom, and I was often puzzled by the kindly, eccentric behaviour of the manager, Tristan Jones, whose father not only knew Lloyd George but had been his parliamentary private secretary. It seemed to me that T.J.

managed by procrastination, something I was unused to. For fifteen years, I had been formulating my own small business policy, making my own decisions and carrying them out. Now I found my ideas interminably held up. In Leeds, I would have thought up an idea over the weekend, and got on with it on Monday. Here at Tudor Street and at Printing House Square, any definition of policy, or prompt action on an issue, seemed to be a totally foreign way of life.

One of my earliest encounters with T.J. came after I had been discussing with the manager of *The Times*, Francis Mathew, some irregularity in the charge they were making for their printing services. On our invoice that week was an item of some £27,000 for three Linotype machines which he said had been bought for the exclusive use of *The Observer*. On one of my walks round the works, I had noticed that the type matrices on these three new machines was something called 4¾ point Claritas. This was a type we never used but it *was* used daily for setting *The Times* stock exchange prices. At first, Mathew argued, but when he saw that I had got the facts right, and was possibly better informed on the subject than he was, he conceded, crossed off the £27,000, and said: 'Worth a try?'

I returned to Tudor Street and went to T.J.'s office to report. The office appeared to be empty. I was about to go away when T.J. popped up from behind his big desk wearing a French gendarme's hat.

'Do you like it?' he asked, pointing to the hat. 'I got it in the Paris Flea Market.'

And then he produced a strange wooden machine consisting of rollers, cog-wheels and a crank handle. It had been used in Luton for crushing straw to make straw hats, a long time ago. This was yet another addition to the vast collection of odd ephemera in T.J.'s private museum in Kent.

Apart from these obsessions with items from the past, T.J. had a deep knowledge of political history, printing and private presses, and an enormous talent for friendship. Eccentric is perhaps an understatement. He had made a ply-wood coffin mounted on pram wheels: at the rear end, actuated by an ingenious arrangement of string, wire and rubber bands, was a plastic hand which waved farewell to the mourners who followed his cortège in June, 1990.

It may have been because I was a technical manager with no writing pretensions that I was so warmly welcomed as soon as I arrived at Tudor Street. The popular image of tough, hard-boiled journalists with green eyeshades seemed far from the true picture. Amongst the writers and sub-editors who became my good friends were Lajos Lederer, our Balkans specialist, who knew Tito; Chris Brasher on the sports desk; Eric Newby, who came in when he was not walking in the Hindu Kush, to write and edit travel pages; John Silverlight, Ken Obank, production editor, and Cliff Hopkinson, picture editor. All contributed to getting out a great newspaper. Cliff recruited the now famous photographer, Donald McCullin, and used some of his first, brilliant press photos.

On the management side, life was not always such a bed of roses. I found it very difficult to get a clear brief out of T.J. or the necessary authority to conduct useful negotiations with the formidable manager of *The Times.* Eventually, after a few cross encounters with T.J. and Holt, I was able to do some effective deals and improve the production of *The Observer* both in quality and quantity.

One Christmas, I found Cliff Hopkinson standing about in Tudor Street after the final edition had gone to press. 'Aunties', the friendly pub on the corner (now, alas, no longer there) had long been closed. I told him it was time he got a cab and went home.

'Not going home,' he muttered, adding some detail about an unhappy domestic situation which he could take no longer.

So I took him home to Twickenham for the night to talk over the problem and provide at least a roof and a meal on Christmas Day. He was great company about the place and a good washer-up. The whole family enjoyed his stay.

When we were packing to go on holiday the following August, I told Cliff that he should really try to find a place of his own. We were glad to have him as a temporary lodger, but he was too old for us to adopt and too young to be a dependent relative. So he found a flat and a new mate.

* * *

I once had a memorable night at *Le Humanité*, the French Communist newspaper in Paris. I had been lecturing on Newspaper Design at the annual conference of Federation Internationale des Editeurs de Journaux et Publications, of which we were members. In the evening, I dropped in at *Le Humanité* which had a very primitive production plant. Coloured ink for a red spot on page one was being slopped on to the rollers from a petrol tin. I found the manager in the canteen on the top floor. We sat on wobbly chairs at crumby tables and started a sort of dialogue with two cups of black coffee. He spoke little English and I, no French, and we had no interpreter, so there was, to say the least, something of a communication problem.

After ten minutes of hand waving and struggling with certain technical phrases common to both tongues, he reached over the counter for a bottle of Cognac and topped up our coffee cups. This he did several times. Soon we discovered that we both had a smattering of soldiers' German, and as the bottle went down, our fluency went up until we were quite at ease with the language of labour relations.

'Are you all communists on the paper?' I asked.

'Yes. All workers are members of the Party.'

'Then you won't have any labour troubles?'

'Monsieur Partridge,' he replied, 'We do not live in 'eaven.'

There was at this time, much talk about colour in newspapers. A Newspaper Colour Association was set up including amongst its international membership: *The Times*, *The Liverpool Post*, *The Milwaukee Journal* and Axel Springer's *Bild Zeitung* – a most improbable assembly. But then, in technical matters, the newspaper industry has no national frontiers. A technical manager is welcomed in any part of the world as a non-competitive comrade with a common interest in producing more and better newspapers.

At *The Times*, Francis Mathew was interested in the colour idea and tried to get *The Observer* to share the capital and development costs for a rotary letterpress colour printing installation to be super-imposed on top of the existing *Times* presses. I opposed this on the grounds that letterpress colour from stereo plates, printed on high-speed newspaper rotary presses, on cheap newsprint by press crews with no training in colour printing and with the press stopping frequently for edition changes, could not be done satisfactorily on a national paper printing a million copies; at least, not for high quality, up-market advertising.

My solution to the colour problem in the 1960's was to get the reels pre-printed by gravure or offset at a plant specialising in colour printing and to run these reels again for the black to be overprinted on a normal newspaper production run. This led me to consider the production problems which would come with the growth of pre-printed colour, the most important of which would be the need for standardisation of page length.

The outcome was that I persuaded *The Observer* and *The Times* to change the length of their pages from 24 inches to 23⁹⁄₁₆ inches, which was beginning to emerge as an international 'standard cut-off'. This meant replacing *The Times* printing presses at a cost of £1.5 million, which would be recovered by newsprint savings from the reduced cut-off and page width. This formula was accepted by both *The Times* and *The Observer.*

What finally happened was that the quality Sunday papers – the *Sunday Times, Sunday Telegraph* and *The Observer* – all started separate gravure printed colour magazines to exploit advertisers' demands for glossy colour. Daily and evening newspapers increasingly used web offset and gravure pre-printed colour, and some provincial weeklies printed offset colour on the run.

I served for a few years on the London Labour Committee of the Newspaper Proprietors Association. This committee was the negotiating body for employers faced with the very powerful Fleet Street unions. The negotiating process was something of a farce or a tragedy, depending on how seriously one took this pistol point, hand-on-switch bargaining. Production managers at the *Financial Times* were told by their directors to be as tough as they liked, provided that the paper didn't miss an edition, which was rather like asking them to take on Mohammed Ali with one hand tied behind their backs. Of course, the unions always won; their wage rates went up to Cabinet Ministers' salary levels, and at no price could co-operation and industrial peace be bought.

Our professional director on the Labour Committee was John Wade, a large, tough barrister, who could give as good as he took in any verbal conflict. The unions respected him because he was formidable and because he could play them at their own game. He could turn on the charm or emit a violent outburst of indignation with a spontaneity which left his colleagues gasping. My guess is that most of the compromise solutions we battled towards in committee had been carved up previously in drinking sessions with the union general secretaries, and that the public show of tough negotiation was as ritualised as a medieval joust. In union vocabulary, to negotiate means to concede. If the employers at any stage dug in their heels, the officials would accuse them of refusing to negotiate.

Partridge Printers Ltd in Leeds was by now employing fifty people with Haydn Scott running the company successfully in his own way, producing excellent work, with very little reference to me. I had a feeling that I had made myself redundant. Both John Waddingtons of Leeds and Weatheroak Press of Birmingham made offers to take us over, which were declined.

In February, 1963, I was approached by Adam Maitland, Managing Director of St. Clements Press — a *Financial Times* subsidiary — in London, to see if I would understudy him with a view to taking over his job in a year's time. I had known Maitland in the Army. He was a major at Bovington Camp when I was teaching radio to Armoured Corps tank crews. St. Clements Press was a large-scale general printing establishment in the City which printed, among other things, the *Financial Times*, *The Economist*, *Amateur Gardening* and several million pounds worth of general publicity and City printing. It consistently lost money and, being in the London Central Branch area of the big unions, and furthermore, printing a national daily newspaper, I could see as an outsider that it would never have a chance of breaking even. Management was by courtesy and consent of the unions.

I was invited to a succession of flattering lunches at the *Financial Times* with the St. Clements Press Chairman, Pat (now Lord) Gibson, and the FT's Chairman, Lord Robbins and its Managing Director, Lord Drogheda.

I told them that St. Clements Press was not a manageable assignment. It would have to be taken apart and got rid of. I would write a paper on how this should be done to achieve a closure without causing labour troubles on the FT. I would find the staff to carry out the plan which would take two to three years to complete. Gibson asked me why I wouldn't do the Managing Director's job myself.

'Haven't you the stomach for it?' he asked, in rather derisory tones.

'You're dead right!' I replied.

And so I joined the board of St. Clements Press with

the agreement of *The Observer.* John Wade was recruited from the NPA to be Managing Director and Alan Cox came from *The Times* to be Works Manager. Meanwhile, I continued to run *The Observer* contract and, by remote control, Partridge Printers.

Soon, Gibson asked me to go into his group full time. The Pearson group controlled the Westminster Press and the *Financial Times*, later acquiring much wider printing and publishing interests, including Penguin Books and the entire Longman publishing business. They offered to buy out Partridge Printers and put it into the Westminster Press Group where I could be chairman of their general printing interests which amounted to a dozen rather ailing commercial print firms.

I discussed the offer with *The Observer* and decided to sell Partridge Printers to the Westminster Press and go into the *Financial Times* as a full-time Technical Manager with a non-executive function as Chairman of the Westminster Press Printing Group. I resigned, finally, from *The Observer* in May, 1964 and moved to an office on the 6th floor of Bracken House, overlooking St. Paul's Cathedral.

3

Grass Roots in Gloucestershire, Norfolk and Yorkshire

I can find no links in my Partridge pedigree with Eric the wordsmith or Bernard the artist; with either of whom or both, I would have been proud to be related. My brother Albert's intensive search in parish registers at Kingswood and Wooton Underedge in Gloucestershire brought no real wealth or fame to light. The Partridges had been broad cloth weavers in this area for many generations. There had been one moment of fame. A certain Captain Partridge – one of us – was hanged at the Tower for being implicated in the Apprentice's Revolt. It was discovered soon after his death that he was completely innocent. He was nowhere near the place at the time. They gave his widow a small property in Devon by way of compensation.

I was the youngest of six children and was greatly loved by my parents, sister and brothers, most of the time, which is probably why I like people in all their unpredictable ways. My father, Frederick Helm Partridge, was the thirteenth child of Henry Partridge of Huddersfield. Only five of the thirteen survived into adult life, the others were taken off mostly by typhoid. My mother was also the thirteenth child, of Charles and

Sarah Mears of East Dereham in Norfolk. By contrast with the Yorkshire family, all thirteen Mears children survived and produced huge families.

Grandfather Mears was a teamsman on a grain farm near East Dereham. He died before I was born. Grandma Mears, I do remember; she came to live with us and our Great Aunt Long, a distinguished looking ex-hospital matron, at the little corner shop my mother kept in Cecil Street, Harrogate.

Charles Mears maintained his team of four horses in superb condition by much grooming and some extra oats, taken in the very early morning before the usual corn ration was issued by the farmer. Charles and Sarah had nine shillings a week on which to bring up their thirteen children. Nine shillings was the Norfolk labourer's wage from 1840 to 1890. Norfolk was not a poor county: only the farm workers were poor. The social pattern was still feudal. The service required of Grandpa's nine shillings included that of all his children. They hoed the fields and scared crows off the corn.

When Grandma was eighty, she sat most of the day in a rocking chair in the kitchen behind the shop. I heard her tell, with an air of cheerfully bold defiance, that when the vicar came to see why her children were not out in the fields – he acted as bailiff and priest – she would tell him they were in bed with coughs. He would demand to see them, but if he so much as stepped over the threshold, Grannie would tell him to get out and threaten him with her umbrella.

Grandpa left the Church of England for the Primitive Methodists, where the parson spoke a language he understood and preached the Gospel as Christ had taught it, without the great ritual and liturgical superstructure imposed by Rome, and sustained by Canterbury over the basic Christian truths.

In 1884, rural workers found themselves, for the first time, admitted to full political rights: a secret ballot and a free vote. When asked, or more likely told, by his employer: 'You'll be voting for my man, Mears?' Charles replied: 'Since the franchise, sir, that's my business.'

You can guess the effect this had on the Squire. It was bad enough to have joined the Methodists, even worse to be a Liberal, but to answer back! That had to be the end. Charles was dismissed and evicted, not only from his cottage, but effectively from the county. Who would now employ this bolshie ranter who had, by expressing his independence, stepped down from the ranks of the 'deserving poor' to join the 'undeserving poor'?

Charles borrowed a cart from the miller and moved with his few belongings, his wife and thirteen children to Hull, where a brother lived. They had been pushed around as much as they were prepared to stand for. Slow to anger, but very obstinate, in the end, they decided to up sticks and make a fresh start away from the feudalism of Norfolk farming.

From Hull, the eight Mears sons went to sea as trawler men, and the five girls went to Bradford to weave alpaca. None of the men learned to swim: it was thought to be unlucky – better to drown quickly than tread water in Icelandic seas and slowly freeze to death. One uncle was drowned off Iceland; two others fell into Immingham Dock and were drowned within three feet of the side. Most of them learned to play the accordion: they would have been better off learning the harp!

Grandfather died soon after they settled in Hull. The cause, according to my mother, who would have been a young girl at the time, was bronchitis. Uncle Sam left the sea, and with his wife, Aunt Sarah, kept the Blue Bell Inn at Cottingham. Aunt Sarah would only serve one pint of beer to men on Fridays unless she was sure that they had taken their wages home to their wives. Another Hull aunt kept a bakery in the Land of Green Ginger where they made ship's biscuits, brandy snap and boiled sweets. Brandy snap was a great favourite to take home from Hull Fair. The ship's biscuits were half an inch thick, five inches square, and had the consistency of old oak floor boards.

Although by this time, we lived at the shop in Harrogate and were used to having plenty of sweets, I will never forget being given almost more than I could carry. It was a huge bag of multi-flavoured, wrapped sweets, soft in the middle and crisp on the outside. I had to use two arms to hold it and put the bag on the ground to get one out to eat. The bag must have weighed five pounds, all slightly sticky; enough to rot the teeth of a nation. But who cared about teeth at the age of eight?!

Great Aunt Long was born at Welborne, in 1840. Her father was Samuel Long and their mother, Rosanna (neé Holly), unable to write her name, made her mark with a cross on the birth certificate. Great Aunt Long had been trained in London as a children's nurse. She became the first matron of Harrogate's first Cottage Hospital and was a distinguished figure and charming old lady when I knew her. She carried herself gracefully, wore high, stiff lace collars, and lived on senna pods and sal volatile. She bought the house, 3 Cecil Street, next to the shop, and a door was knocked through between the two front bedrooms, so that I could baffle my friends from lower down the street by appearing in the front bedroom window of No. 1, above the shop, and then, almost instantly, in the bedroom window of No. 3, which by all the laws of street architecture must involve running downstairs and out the back door of No. 1 and into No. 3 before making this dramatic appearance from behind the lace curtains in Great Aunt Long's bedroom.

After she retired from the Cottage Hospital, Great Aunt Long kept a boarding house to which a Sir William and Lady Waterlow came as guests. Very up-market! My mother and Aunt Annie left the Bradford mills and came to work for Great Aunt Long in Harrogate. Aunt Rosie was a maid there, too. One of Rosie's suitors walked over from Bradford to see her. Arriving back in Bradford, footsore and exhausted, he kicked off his boots and said, 'Niver agean, not for noa Rosies'.

Auntie Annie married William Cooper of Bradford. He loved singing, as did many working people in the West Riding. Singing and drinking were his downfall, we were solemnly warned. I think Annie walked out on him; they had no children. Will Cooper came from another large family who also lived in two houses knocked into one. They were all musical and had many choral and orchestral friends. When friends called for one or other of the boys or girls and asked if they were in, their mother would say: 'I'm sure I don't know if 'e's in. Come in and 'ave a lewk raand.'

Aunt Fanny was an adopted aunt. She was Annie's partner in the guest houses they ran in Harrogate. Fanny was tall and thin, wore pince-nez and jet beads. She ran the business and Annie was the cook. Old Hooker King, Fanny's father, came from Norfolk to Harrogate with Fanny and her brothers and sister. When I knew him, he was an out-porter at the station and a Bath chair man.

He met the trains and trundled a huge porter's barrow full of cases round the town for commercial travellers: before they had cars, they moved around with what was no less than a portable showroom on Hooker's barrow, calling on shops and displaying their wares. He was still doing this in 1925 when I started work but as cars came in, out-portering went out. I also remember his wicker Bath chair. He stood on a Bath chair rank opposite the Prospect Hotel, waiting to be summoned by the hotel porters and, tucking in rheumatic old ladies and gentlemen with large plaid rugs, he wheeled them gently down to the Pump Room for their daily drinks of obnoxious sulphur or magnesia water.

Apart from the shop, Grove Road Chapel was the centre of our lives. Some or all of us went to Chapel or Sunday School twice every Sunday and it was half an hour's walk each way. There were meetings on many nights in the week, socials and outings which were great fun and our parents' only form of social relaxation in an otherwise hard, grinding week.

One minister used to announce in September that on such and such a Saturday afternoon, there would be 'ay nutting expedition', with the emphasis on the hard 'g'. This would be a three or four mile walk through the country to Beckwithshaw Chapel where tea, and of course, buns, would be provided. The 'nutting' meant gathering usually unripe hazelnuts from the hedges on the way. I can still taste the bitter-sweet, pithy, soft-shelled green nuts with kernels like orange pips. But the tea, buns and games at Beckwithshaw were a delightful source of innocent merriment for all of us, from the very young to those of the elderly who could still amble four miles and climb a stile.

Grove Road Chapel had a good orchestra in which my brother, Clifford, played Grandpa's violin; there was also a choir in which he sang bass and my sister, Hilda, sang contralto. I can remember not a word that was ever uttered from the pulpit except, perhaps, that the wages of sin is death, but I can remember the words and music of most of the anthem solo parts that were sung by our leading soprano, Jessie Hewson, and the heady tenor, Mr Duffy, which makes me think that all teaching would be more memorable if set to music and sung.

At the socials, young and old took part in sketches which didn't quite warrant the name amateur theatricals, although they were very amateur and very comical. Our mothers played domestic farces which made some of the more formidable matrons seem a little more human to us children. We were delighted to see dignity unbuttoned. The young men and women dressed up for their parts and were allowed to indulge in slightly rude frivolity. I played the Irish servant boy in the Sunday School performances with which we toured the district. I was completely absorbed in my own part and never saw it really as part of a whole performance with others. I was a deeply embarrassed, pink-faced thirteen year-old when big girls at other Chapels would shout, 'Does your mother know you're out?' as I stepped from the stage and walked through the schoolroom to where the eternal tea and buns were provided.

My father, Fred, was born in Huddersfield in 1867. He went to Ackworth School with his elder brother, John, where they studied Euclid, Latin and the pianoforte. It seems to have been an unhappy, best-forgotten time for my father. He played some cricket and must have been a wicket keeper because he had a permanent blue bruise on the back of one thumb which he said was from an injury he got behind the wicket. One letter remains from the Victorian father (my grandfather) to his schoolboy son. It is formal and without a sign of affection although, when I read it now, I sense a father remote and responsible, yet unable rather than unwilling to introduce any single expression of love or tenderness for his fifteen year old youngest child. It was written in Fred's last term and it advised him that he should now set out to learn a trade; this would ensure a living and security. Arrangements had been made for him to be apprenticed to Wallace's, an early multiple store with several grocery shops in the West Riding.

Father served his apprenticeship at a Wallace's shop which was open from 8 a.m. to 8 p.m. daily and until nine or ten in the evening on Saturdays. The manager's discipline was harsh: the staff was 'on parade' for as long as there was anyone in the shop. Goods hung outside could not be taken in if there was any possible customer in the street. Father would often tell of some boarding-house keeper who always came at closing time and would buy a whole ham, then ask for it to be sliced thinly. This was done by hand with great skill and it took a long time, but all the assistants had to stay and look alert until the last customer had gone.

From Wallace's, father went to work at John Wood's, a fashionable Grocer, Tea Blender and Italian Warehouseman in James Street, Harrogate. John Wood and his wife were in the classic tradition of Victorian traders who imported not only confections from Italy and ginger from China, but also pottery and vases from the Orient which were displayed in a side window with other objets d'art. They served the County or carriage trade. Ladies in carriages drew up at the shop front and the manager, Charles Greaves, would take their orders at the carriage, his long, fringed apron, spotless, brushing his polished toe caps. The butler from the Duke of Devonshire's Bolton Abbey estate came to order at John Wood's. Father or Mr. Greaves went by pony trap to the Dales, buying hams and cheeses from farms, first sampling them with a hollow skewer, with which they took a taste from the middle.

As secretary, Miss Greaves, Charles Greaves' daughter, kept the accounts, but Father graduated to Chief Clerk or 'Bookkeeper' as we always described him on school forms which asked for his occupation. Bookkeeper sounded pretty good. Some extraordinary characters worked at John Wood's. One old delivery man who looked after the horse and van always appeared so poverty stricken that customers gave him cast-off clothing. When he failed to turn up one day, old Collinson, a kindly counter assistant, went to find him in his slum cottage in Ship Yard to see if he had overslept. He found the old man dead in bed in a room piled high with old clothing, and a tin box containing seven hundred gold sovereigns under his bed.

The carriage trade fell off in Harrogate as other more modern shops – Standing's, Farrah's and the Imperial Cafe – set up in competition. John Wood never forgave Standing for a trick played when a property at the Station end of James Street came on the market. Wood would have liked to have it but it was expected to fetch too high a price for him. He canvassed his main rival – Standing – who said he would keep out of the bidding; then, behind Wood's back, Standing made a private deal and bought the property in which he set up competition.

It was not competition, however, that put an end to John Wood's shop. When the old man died, his son, George Wood, a solicitor, sold it three times over to unsuspecting old ladies whose affairs he was supposed to be looking after. He was tried for fraud and died in Armley Gaol before completing a seven year sentence. Mrs. Wood died of grief, and the business came to an end. My father was the youngest employee. He was just over sixty and had given near on forty years' service. Charles Greaves had been with the firm for fifty-two years. The door was locked behind them without a handshake.

For sixty years up to the 1914 war, and possibly after it into the 'twenties, Harrogate was a smart and fashionable spa. The prosperity of the town was largely dependent on the Pump Room and the Royal Baths, well supported by a range of splendid hotels which, in the season, were full of the elegant, the gouty and the senile. Well-to-do farmers from Scotland were wheeled from the station in Bath chairs to undergo a course of treatment consisting of a strict diet: no alcohol, lots of magnesia or sulphur water and massages which apparently worked wonders on their seized-up joints and hob-nailed livers. They stuck religiously to the 'treatment' until mobile enough to stagger down to Hale's Vaults, an excellent period pub close to the Pump Room where they would cast discipline aside and go back to Johnny Walkers and Glen Livett. At the end of the 'treatment', they would be wheeled back to the station in the same state in which they arrived.

Harrogate was a class-conscious town where everyone knew his place. Rich people lived in Duchy Road or Kent Road. Anyone we came across using a long 'a' as in 'barth' or 'graass' would be said to be talking Duchy Road. Professional people lived in large Pateley stone houses facing onto The Stray, 200 acres of common land, mown like a lawn, and preserved for public use 'without let or hindrance'. The working classes lived in streets and terraces in Bilton, New Park and other estates built for the lower orders. We were in Bilton.

4

Childhood in World War One. Printers' Devil using Caxton's Methods

For you know, dear — I may, without vanity, hint —
Though an angel should write, still 'tis *devils* must print.

Thomas Moore, 1779–1852

I WAS BORN on Friday, August 18th, 1911, at 37 Cecil Street, Harrogate, just before midnight. The hymn, *Brightest and best are the 'sons' of the morning*, has always bothered me.

We moved to the shop at No. 1 Cecil Street when I was one year old, Aunts Annie and Fanny having taken over a classy boarding house, 'Heatherdene', in Harlow Moor Drive. My earliest memory is of being in the kitchen behind the shop, strapped in a high chair, which folded down into a rocking chair by an ingenious linkage of spring clips and hinges, roaring my head off while Mother was in the shop selling rusks to Mrs. Rankin for her Leslie. I am quite clear in my memory that I didn't at all like my mother spending so much time in the shop. It stood between her and me and I resented it bitterly.

Father worked at John Wood's all the time we had the shop. His weekly wage rose to 70 shillings from 1916 to 1918, when shop assistants were scarce, but was cut back to 60 shillings in 1919 when returning soldiers came on the labour market. Keeping Father protected as far as possible, Mother ran the shop at the same time as bringing up six children and looking after aged aunts, grannies and sick relatives. The shop, she said, gave us a bit better 'going on' than we would have had just on Father's wage.

Cecil Street had about twenty-five houses on each side with stone fronts, slate roofs and brick backs. It was one of seven or eight similar parallel streets housing the hotel workers, joiners, plumbers and shop assistants. Cecil Street was first in the social order, however, being nearest to Church Avenue and King Edward's Drive, which were relatively middle class; or upper-working, anyway. The shop was not only a shop but an end house, with cellars and a larger front bedroom than any of the other houses in the street.

Richard Hoggart comments on the social superiority bestowed by an end-of-terrace house in his book, 'A Local Habitation' (Chatto & Windus, 1988). Thus, our status was reinforced not only by Great Aunt Long's position as hospital matron, and Annie and Fanny running a posh boarding house, but street-wise as well.

We were always well-shod and well-dressed by local standards. Butler Roaders from the other end of the block of streets might take charity from the *Yorkshire Post*'s 'Boots for the Bairns' fund. We dispensed charity – at Chapel and the back door. Mother said it was better to give to nine scroungers than to refuse one deserving case. It was a family tradition to give and not to accept charity. Grandma Mears, who needed help with her brood if ever anyone did, was far too proud to take help and never let it be seen how poor she really was. Her family were always turned out well-darned and with no shirt showing through the seats of pants, and no 'potatoes' at sock heels.

The shop was really a converted front room, about twelve feet square, including window bottom, where dead wasps lay on their backs just out of reach. The cellar underneath was approached either through the kitchen or by a heavy trap door on the shop front, down which Sidney Fisher fell when he was little and was thereafter known as Cellar Fisher. There were incandescent gas mantles in the shop and in the kitchen, and on the landing at the top of the stairs, a batswing burner flared noisily with a blue flame and yellow penumbra. Paraffin, potatoes and bundles of sticks were stored in the cellar; bread under the mahogany counter; butter and bacon on one shelf; patent medicines, friar's balsam, cherry flavoured cough mixture in half gallon bottles, sweet nitre, tincture of quinine and senna pods, on another. Not many foodstuffs were pre-packed. Tea, flour and sugar were weighed up and packeted on Wednesday afternoons, butter and bacon and treacle were weighed and measured out as customers waited and gossiped in the shop. We sold paper blinds and sweets: everlasting strips, spanish bootlaces, tiger nuts, monkey nuts, love whispers and pear drops.

We children were well off at the shop with its cellars beneath and hen run in the yard. Mother kept a pet bantam cock and a few pullets. She once chopped off the head of an old rooster, prior to plucking it for Sunday dinner, and the headless body took off and raced three times round the backyard.

We were never short of friends; like all boys, we fell out and made up frequently. A permanent feud raged between Cecil Streeters and Butler Roaders. This reached explosion point at bonfire time when, to protect our bonfire piles, we dug trenches and mounted guard until late at night against the barbarian hoards from the rough end of Bilton. Clay fights and stone-throwing went on from deep-dug trenches, but I don't remember many serious casualties. I was treated for burns when someone threw a Chinese cracker that went down the back of my neck, and for cuts when I put an Andrew's Liver Salts tin over a flash bomb which went off before I did.

I ran a very exclusive club in our hen house. It was limited to four members, the maximum number that could crouch in at the same time. We laughed a lot, quarrelled and made up. Like the Reform Club in Pall Mall which I joined later, it was for male members only.

In front of the shop counter were cases of pop bottles from Barraclough's Mineral Water Works. Arthur, a curly-headed, local child, stole bottles of pop while Mother was in the cellar getting paraffin, and brought the empties back for a penny on the bottle next day. He was brought up by his Aunt Maggie and used to steer her home from the Dragon pub through the muddy streets with Maggie moaning, 'Arthur, I'm in it again', as she stumbled in the puddles.

The police came to school one day looking for Arthur and we were all told to find him and bring him to the police station. Twelve of us, led by Jimmy Bland, chased the wretched lad out of his hiding place in Bilton fields and handed him over to Police Constable Blanchflower. I felt sorry for Arthur and was afraid to catch him but more afraid not to join in the hunt. I have never forgiven myself even though, at the time, I thought he shouldn't have pinched pop from our shop. He was without malice and unloved except by his forlorn Aunt Maggie.

One child came into the shop for a pound of treacle which was run out of a square tank with gold lettering into his jam jar. When asked for his money, the boy said it was in the jar and sure enough, there was a bright six-pence at the bottom of the dark treacle.

Tommy Rankin, who managed the local office of the *Yorkshire Post*, always asked for his corned beef to be cut 'with a hammy knife to give it a flavour'. Pearl Gardener, a young lady from a family in reduced circumstances, who spoke with a conspicuously elegant accent, would ask for some 'really frilling jam' and spend minutes choosing between blackberry and greengage.

The kitchen behind the shop was nearly filled by a large, round table which sat six comfortably and ten at a pinch. There was a piano, and a black and bright steel fireplace bearing the nameplate 'Hudsons Ironworks' with a side oven, in front of which the bread was put to rise in a large earthenware bowl on baking days.

Father's desk was on one side of the fireplace and the pot cupboard on the other. The lower shelf of the pot cupboard housed the first radio I ever heard. It was built by my brother, Freddie, and cousin, Billy Atkinson. First it was a crystal set, then a one-valve detector plus valve amplifier. Headphones were put in a pudding basin so that more of us could hear the faint signals from 2LO: Captain P.P. Eckersley, The Savoy Orpheans and John Henry.

The desk was a place of less happy memories. This was where Father would make up the books at night, and at the month's end, decide which bills could be paid. It is impossible to say whether any profits were ever made. Neighbours said the shop was a 'little gold mine'. The best Mother would say was that we were better fed, better clothed than most of our neighbours and were undoubtedly better off than the Mears family had been in Norfolk.

In the early days, the shop must have helped us quite a

lot, but later, as the co-ops and many other small shops set up in the district, I'm sure it was poor reward for all the hard work and worry that went into it. I saw my mother in tears when she could not pay the wholesalers' bills on time; but we children were sheltered from anxieties of this sort.

Saturdays at Cecil Street were rag-time days, happy days, when we sang songs about the house which I remember as Saturday songs, such as *Alexander's Rag-time Band*, *Swannee River* and *Any Old Iron.* Sundays were solemn days: no Sunday papers were allowed in the house, nor could we buy ice cream penny cornets or twopenny sandwiches from old Carola's barrow which he pushed round the streets. The routine was Chapel, dinner, Sunday School and Chapel again for most of us. But on Sunday nights, our house would be full of friends singing parts of *The Messiah* or Gilbert and Sullivan choruses; even the comic patter songs were allowed and greatly enjoyed.

One Sunday night in 1916 as we were walking home from Chapel, a Zeppelin floated overhead, lit up by a searchlight's beam. There were no anti-aircraft batteries in our district so to frustrate the enemy and keep our spirits up, we all joined in and sang 'Singing to welcome the pilgrims of the night'.

As children, when we had bronchitis, we were taken to the New Park gas works to smell the gas tar, the local old wives' cure for all chest ailments. Slums, on the scale of other northern towns, did not exist in Harrogate but one or two streets declined into fringe slummery. Denmark Street was one such street. It contained the local doss house run by Carola, the town's first Italian ice cream man whose large family pushed their barrows around the streets. It was fourpence a night at Carola's doss house. He was said to get his lodgers to sleep on a bed then prop them up against the wall to make room for latecomers.

The war was very much on our minds as children. England was never in the front line then as London and other cities were during the Battle of Britain, but the tragedies of the First World War were never far away. Extreme patriotism was generated through the Press and the hoardings: 'Your King and Country need You' declaimed the severe face and pointing finger of Lord Kitchener – and the young men went, and died in their thousands. I was a three-year-old toddler when the conflict started and seven at the end of this 'war to end all wars'.

We had two wounded soldiers billetted with us at Cecil Street: Mr Davy and Mr Diapre were kindly men, very much at ease in our house. When we heard military bands in the distance, we ran up to Skipton Road to watch the soldiers march by on their way to Killinghall camp. At school, we had apple day, potato day and carrot day; each child being asked to bring one fruit or vegetable for the wounded soldiers. It was a great honour to be asked to wheel the barrow of carrots to the hospital and talk to the men in hospital blue.

Henry, my eldest brother, was born in 1900. He went to the Grammar School and then worked in the Council offices. All his friends began to join the Services in 1917, and at seventeen years of age, tall, fair and quiet spoken, Henry went to join up as well. But he was not old enough – he had to be eighteen – so the Recruiting Officer said: 'Take a walk round the Town Hall, lad, and have a birthday on the way'. So Henry did this and came back five minutes later, a year older.

He trained for six weeks at Christchurch and then

went out as a pilot-observer. Within three months, he was shot down and died of wounds in Flushing, Holland, where he is buried. The War Office telegram came to the shop one morning. I didn't see the tragic message but saw Mother sobbing bitterly and supporting herself on the towel that hung behind the scullery door. I clung to her apron and cried, too. She asked why I was crying. I couldn't answer so she answered for me: 'Is it because I am crying?' I nodded, and we wept together.

My years from the age of ten to fourteen are full of memories of school, street gangs and Bilton Woods. We attended school only half-time during the war because so many of the male teachers were in the Army. I had successive crushes on the prettier female teachers. After the war, we had very good teachers from the Services: Long Pullan, Dingy Horner, Hinde Leedale, Chalky White and Mawson, the headmaster, whose morning ritual included the entire school reciting in chorus after him: 'Con-cen-tra-shun, put cher mind on wot cher doing', which is the only part of morning prayers I can remember. He put a lot of emotion into it, and the two 'chers' exploded on Class One in the front row, like the spray from a water pistol.

In Bilton Woods, we dodged the keeper and explored forbidden areas. Geoff Langham, Harry Thrower and Norman Wilkinson were my companions. We climbed the tall pine trees in search of owls' nests, with sheath knives in our mouths as protection against the parent birds, but mainly for dramatic effect. We dug a mantrap to catch the keeper but never found him dying and pleading for mercy in the pit, which was at least two foot six inches deep. I fell in love with a girl across the river at Scotton Mills; she was probably a princess, but I couldn't reach her or even talk to her for the noise of the water rushing over the broken weir. So I threw her my orange on two Saturdays as tokens of love. When the school holidays ended, she went away, and I never even knew her name.

Geoff Langham and I used to walk down Bilton fields on one side of the hedge, while on the other side, walked the two fair Dyson twins, daughters of a taxi driver. At an unspoken signal, we all lay down, crept towards each other and kissed for a few pulsating moments.

At hay time in the fields, there was a lot of pushing, tumbling and fumbling between the boys and girls, but from twelve or thirteen onwards, girls were a problem and kissing became something to be avoided if at all possible. We took our girlfriends to the Saturday afternoon cinema collectively; three or four boys and roughly the same number of girls, but separated into our monastic brotherhoods afterwards.

I left school on the last Friday in July, 1925, and started work on the first Tuesday in August as errand boy for A.R. Baines, optician and camera shop in James Street: nine shillings a week, 8.30 am to 6 pm, finishing at 1 pm on Saturdays. By my fourteenth birthday, I had been working for two weeks.

I swept the shop, cleaned the windows, delivered parcels to the big houses, hotels and schools, washed up the wine glasses after morning gin sessions attended by the boss's friends and brought in afternoon tea on a tray from the Imperial Cafe, walking often through a gale of wind and rain across Prospect Square, trying not to spill the milk. The waitresses gave me cakes for myself, and their friendly teasing caused erections, helped by the tray rubbing on my penis. Much later, when I worked in

Leeds, Mike Hooley, our apprentice, said, 'Boy, if you haven't wanked, you haven't lived', showing that there were two points of view on the guilt-ridden question of masturbation.

The General Strike and the depression of the late 'twenties were already on the horizon. One of the regular callers for a drink at the shop in James Street, a little man called Butterfield, was in cotton. His pals cheered him up by reciting:

> 'Poor bloody Butterfield, he's in a hole
> No bloody money, no bloody coal.
> Now't in the pantry, no bloody dole.
> Who'll buy his cotton shares?
> Not a damned soul.'

Shunning the Boy Scouts and organised youth clubs, a dozen of us – errand boys, young shop assistants and mechanics – started a health and strength club in a rented room above a garage. The subscription was sixpence or a shilling a week, according to age and income. We boxed and weight-lifted and went for long Sunday walks. Wilkinson was our pocket Hercules with 'muscles like an ox and a back like a table' as the saying went. We had some good amateur boxers. I had a few fights in public in a ring put up on the tennis courts of the Woodlands Hotel. When I was broken, nose and tooth, by battering-ram blows from a youth who had been an Army lightweight champion, I gave it up and let my putty nose resume something like its normal shape. The promoter, Mr Cann, said as I walked back to the dressing room for the last time: 'Lovely left, classic style, could have gone a long way – but too much the little gentleman.'

When I had been an errand boy at the optician's for a year, I thought this was long enough and started to look for a trade. As Grandfather had said, the thing was to have a skilled trade in your hands – no-one could take that from you. I fancied joinering as I was useful with tools and loved to see the grain in wood change pattern under the sharp blade of a plane. I was offered a job at Stevenson's, carriage builders, but turned it down when I noticed that the firm were also undertakers. Then a short, fat, asthmatic old man called Parkinson, a printing manager from York who stayed with my aunties at the boarding house, suggested I should be a printer. He knew an ink salesman called Fisher who would look out for a job for me which he did, quickly and successfully.

Ben Thorpe had been a compositor at Ackrill's, the Harrogate newspaper owners and largest general printers in the district. Ben was a cheerful, curly-haired compositor with a fine bass voice. He was choirmaster at Knaresborough Catholic Church and it was his custom to go to Wetherby races every Easter Tuesday for some after-Lent refreshment of the spirit. The manager at Ackrill's was a Mr. Breare and at Easter in 1926, he took it into his head to post a notice announcing that anyone who absented himself from work on Easter Tuesday would be sacked. Ben Thorpe was not a man to let a little thing like this interfere with his long-standing appointment with the turf. And so on the Wednesday, he was fired. With a couple of hundred pounds from his savings and a whip-round by the 'chapel' (union branch) at Ackrill's, Ben set up shop in Strawberry Vale, in the front sitting-room of a Victorian terraced house owned by Mr. Billington, a house painter. I was Ben's first and only apprentice. The plant consisted of an Arab platen, which I treadled for the first six months, a hand lever guillotine, a hand stitcher and about sixty cases of type. When we got a one horse-power motor to drive the platen, I really saw this as a great step forward in mechanisation.

Ben was a good craftsman compositor and taught me well. When he was out, I drew girls' heads on scrap paper as I watched them walk by. When Ben came in, he, too, would watch and admire the girls.

'That one would do to practice on,' he would say, pointing out to me some busty tart with her chin up and chest out, and I would burst into roars of laughter. I was 'the best laugher in the northern union' he often said.

We printed billheads, cards, tickets, programmes and booklets. Type formes were occasionally borrowed by stealth from the back door of Ackrill's, Ben's erstwhile employers, if we got a job that he knew they had standing. This gave us the competitive edge over all the other local printers – including Ackrill's. The type was returned after we had printed the job.

In 1927, Ben Thorpe went to an auction at Knaresborough and for £300, bought the old, established printing firm of Geo. Wood, Finkle Street. Geo. Wood had died and his son, Fred, had not managed to keep the business going successfully. When Ben took over, Fred stayed on as our journeyman. Now there was Ben, Fred and me, with Ben's daughter, Marjorie, coming in to help with the Auction Mart Catalogue once a week.

The printing works was through a brick archway on the north side of Finkle Street and up wooden stairs over the yard and warehouse of Petch and Co., corn and potato merchants. Up the stairs, you first came to the ink shelves and the tall cupboard where rollers for the quad crown Wharfedale were kept. The place had a heavy scent of ink, mouldy paste, coke fumes, rancid rollers, gas from the leaky gas engine bellows and mouse droppings. Mice frequented the roller cupboard and nibbled the roller ends which were made of glycerine, treacle and gelatine. The big roller cupboard door was thick with the paste of ages, where the edge of cylinder dressing sheets and the tympan sheets of the old hand press had been pasted.

Dead paste hung like wax down a candle bottle, coloured in black, red and green drools, resembling a Jackson Pollock painting, from the dripping ink tins and splashes when rollers were leaned up for washing with ink-soaked paraffin rags. A seven horse-power gas engine drove the two printing machines through festoons of belting and counter shafts which spanned the room.

Arnold Bennett's description of the Bursley printing office in his book, *Clayhanger*, gives an almost exact picture of our Knaresborough printing works, except that the floor did not threaten to collapse and our source of power to drive the cylinder press was not steam but a monstrous gas engine which I decarbonised on Monday mornings, unbracketing the big-end bearing and withdrawing the heavy piston.

To start the beast, I would prime it with petrol and then swing the four foot fly wheel, letting go fast and leaping out of the way when it backfired. The Arab platen, work horse of small printers in every town in the country at this time, was driven either by treadle or gas engine. The big machine was a quad crown Wharfedale cylinder press by Payne of Otley with stick flyers and wooden cylinder bearers. When the cylinder needed trueing-up, we sent for a joiner who made a new pair of bearers in well-seasoned oak with nicely countersunk screw holes.

The third press was not power driven. It was a double crown Columbian hand press with a large, iron, bald eagle perched on the counter-poise lever. This press had its hundredth birthday in Knaresborough while I was working it. The Columbian press was first introduced into this country by a Mr. Clymer of Philadelphia in 1817. We used ours for pulling proofs and short runs of posters.

If William Caxton had turned up looking for work with us at Finkle Street in Knaresborough, it would have taken him no more than an hour or two to fall in line with what we were doing and earn his keep. We set everything from cases of loose type and printed proofs and posters on a Columbian hand press which was an iron development of Caxton's own 'common' wooden press with a 'great lever' added by George Clymer to increase its power. He may have needed a little more instruction on the old Wharfedale press and the gas engine, but type setting and page make-up would have been no bother at all.

Our orders were typical of a small country town jobbing printer: auctioneers' posters and catalogues, the parish magazine, stationery and cards, and occasionally a guidebook. All our setting was done by hand from heavy cases of Miller and Richards or Caslon type. I could soon set a thousand ens an hour; Ben could do more. Fred could, but wouldn't. Ben and I sang as we set. He would give me the treble line in one of the madrigals he was rehearsing with his choir. I would know it well enough by the second time through, then he would plunge into the bass part:

Ben. Bass:	'The steeds in their stalls stamp and neigh when they hear the ostler call'
Me. Treble:	'The Tide Rises'

The factory inspector, Miss McEwan, was either blind or benevolent. The only thing she seemed to insist on was a hot water supply. Ours was cold from a tap in the yard but by standing the bucket on the iron coke stove, we always got it warm enough to placate 'Miss Factory Acts', as we called her. Glue for bookbinding was boiled up and tea was brewed on the coke stove. In winter on really cold days, we had a large glug of rum in our tea in the mornings, which helped the singing no end. We grew tomatoes on the composing room window ledge. They grew up tall and spindly to the light but produced some nice fruit, helped on by a mulch of horse manure from the yard below.

Ben Thorpe kept his accounts in a Boots' diary. At best, he broke even on the year, but competition was keen; prices were low and profit was very hard to earn. The situation was not helped by the fact that Ben had little idea about selling or costing. When we quoted for Council work, he always said our estimates were leaked by the Town Clerk to our rivals, Parr's Printers, before their price went in. It seemed more than coincidental that so often their price was just ten shillings below ours on jobs worth a hundred pounds, and that Parr's manager and the clerk to the Council were both freemasons. Ben was a Catholic. I have never to this day rid myself of a deep-rooted distaste and suspicion of all things masonic.

After six years, Ben could not get enough work out of Knaresborough to make it worthwhile staying there, so we moved back to Harrogate, leaving, without regrets, the stinking gas engine and the ancient quad crown Wharfedale press. He rented an even smaller works and tried unsuccessfully to sell stationery as well as print. One day, he told me sadly that the business could not stand my wages. I was out of my time and twenty-two. So I went to work for Walter Ogden and his wife at the Electric Press behind Symmington's Book Shop in Market Square, Harrogate: a most eccentric establishment.

The Ogdens said that they couldn't afford to pay me the full union rate of £3.7.6d. so I accepted £2.10s. a week and the promise of a share of the profits at the year end. The Electric Press had the same plant as the Knaresborough works: an Arab platen, a quad crown Wharfedale, a hand operated stitcher and guillotine, all of antique vintage. The work was similar: posters, catalogues, programmes and stationery for Walter's brother, James R. Ogden, Court Jeweller.

James was short and fat; the brighter brother of the two, he was an amateur Egyptologist as well as a famous jeweller, and had been involved in the excavation of Tutankhamen's tomb. Walter, on the other hand, was comic, simple and incredibly thin; his alpaca jacket hung from his shoulder blades like a shirt on a coathanger. We worked amicably together for a few months. Walter tripped about like Jack Point, finger pointing forward as he hopped and skipped to answer the doorbell, welcoming some surprised salesman with a deep bow and wide flourish of his left arm. Every movement had a Gilbertian air and, if he had been a bit cleverer, I have no doubt that his vocation would have been in comic opera. As it was, he was more than content with a small part in the local Operatic Society productions. We read proofs in phonetic language: 'Antique Ma-ho-gan-i Pea-des-tal'.

I fed the jeweller's stationery or the fishmonger's labels into the insatiable Arab platen; stroked the pile forward with the right thumb nail, took up the edge with the thumb pad and two fingers while withdrawing and stacking the printed sheet with the left hand, fed in the blank sheet and stroked it home to the lay pins with a second finger of the right hand. I repeated this motion ten thousand times a day at 1,250 impressions an hour for interminable days and weeks. To stave off melancholy, I used to pin up poetry on the wall and see how many lines of Ralph Waldo Emerson I could learn to each thousand sheets printed. It was Emerson because he was available: the paper merchants, Grosvenor Chater, printed his work on their paper samples.

At the year's end, there was no profit to share out so I continued my journey.

5

Journeyman and Soldier. A Swiss Romance

When we left the shop I missed my back street friends but soon found new ones in a cycling club. Every weekend we explored the tracks and byeways of the Yorkshire Dales and the Lake District; we went on holiday tours around Scotland, Wales and Norway, avoiding flat country and concentrating on the mountains.

The shop had become too much of a worry for my mother and was no longer profitable so it was sold – house, shop and stock-in-trade, for £400. Our new home, a grey stone, three-storey house near the Valley Gardens cost precisely the same amount, £400. How times change, and what a dramatic effect inflation has had on property values. Father got a part-time job and Mother let rooms to help make a living.

I went to the Leeds College of Printing on three evenings a week, eventually getting a first class honours in City and Guilds typography. On a non-school night, I sang in the local amateur operatics or discussed next week's cycling trip with my mates. We generally avoided girls although, in the Spring, some of the boys did break out and race the sixty-eight miles to Kendal with, as they boasted, a box of chocolates in one pocket and a French letter in the other. The return trip, known as a knee shaker, was always something of an ordeal unless there was a following west wind to help the satiated but not disillusioned Don Juans over Blubberhouses Moor on the way home.

The rest of us laughed at these exploits, moving from Buckden to Hawes, or Hawes to Reeth, in order not to get too involved with the daughters of the farmhouses where we ate and slept at weekends. Golden opportunities were wasted but we greatly feared the ball and chain of a steady courtship and were, in fact, very ignorant of, and certainly embarrassed by, the whole love-making procedure. We courted by Christmas card, saw our local girlfriends on wet Saturdays two or three times in winter, but never in summer, and carried on romantic love with remote females at safe distances, singing the summer days away in the Dales and Lakes with folk ballads and Schubert lieder. One by one, we grew up and married in our late twenties.

Our bicycles were made by Fred Smith in his clean-swept workshop in Ripon, where the benches were covered with the white sheets of a Morning Post. Bicycle parts, axles, forks and ball-bearing races were arranged in an orderly display on the walls. With half an inch of cigarette singeing a grey moustache, ponderous shoulders wheezing up and down, Mr. Smith trued-up the spokes of a bicycle wheel with the dexterity of a piano tuner. He was thorough and slow; always tired, always happy to put down his work and talk. He was one of a now almost extinct breed of craftsmen-traders. Even when a customer knew what he wanted, was prepared to wait for it, and pay for it, Fred still raised every possible objection.

'I am encountering enormous difficulty in obtaining

good materials,' he would complain. 'You cannot possibly have it for June. All the Accles and Pollock quality tubing must be going into armaments.'

Special customers would be ushered through the shop and into the works by Mrs. Smith, who looked like Queen Victoria. The visitor enters. Mr. Smith puts down his tools, lights another cigarette from the old tab-end and steers the conversation from what the customer wants, to politics, newspaper production, antique faking or pacifism, quack medicine or Mendelssohn. We all enjoyed his little parliament, especially Mr. Smith.

My first job in Leeds was with a one-man press in Garden Green, Holbeck, about as far from a garden as you can get in the West Riding, and never green. It was at the back of Holbeck Station. I remember flagstone pavements greasy with wet soot, and endless battered dustbins. The platen press was in an upstairs room, as were so many little printing shops. It was owned by a man who worked in the Leeds city Rates Office. He got orders for printing from tradespeople, I was told, by 'helping' to get their rates reduced. Actually, I think he did this by fiddling the books. He had a schoolboy son, an insufferable twit, and the idea was to build up a little business for the boy. Most of the jobs were for tradesmen's stationery. I stuck it for about three weeks.

Next I went to Trinity Press where the boss, Mr. Hayden, liked the designs I sent in with my application and set me on at once as a display compositor. He really didn't have enough work to keep me employed full-time; it was full-time for about two weeks, then short time. This was no good so I moved again – to Richard Sissons. One Friday, Mr. Sissons couldn't pay my wages which were £3.7.6d. for a full week but actually we were on short time, earning about fifty-five shillings. He asked if I would take his old motor bike in lieu of wages to save my bus fares. This was not to my liking so I was off again, first as a compositor and a month later, as foreman at Kemps Directories, East Street, Leeds. This remarkable outfit ended up at the Old Bailey.

Being the foreman at Kemps was an interesting job while it lasted. I was twenty-three, and it was the first time I had been in charge of men. There were two machine men and an apprentice, three night operators and three day operators on linotypes, one case hand and apprentice; the bindery was farmed out and the office staff were housed remotely up a flight of stairs. We turned out enormous quantities of setting and printing with this small staff. David Ryder, Charlie Kearsley and Cecil Ray were quick, clean typesetters who worked fast and made few mistakes. Cecil was an ex-jockey, and his father a well-known jockey and trainer. David was responsible, later on, for getting me my first job in newspapers at the *Daily Mail* in Manchester where he became the head printer, an appointment he held until his retirement in 1979.

At lunchtime, we ate our sandwiches in the machine room and performed pantomime sketches, like the one about rescuing the maiden from the tower. One of the apprentices, Mike Hooley, would be the maiden and one of the others would plod round and round him to the 'top' of the tower, pick him up and step round and round again in the other direction down the 'tower'. This was the source of much innocent merriment. But R.D.Whipple, the boss, didn't think so. He had me in the office and complained that I was 'too familiar with the men'. I was frightened of Whipple with his thick neck and waddling gait so I reacted aggressively and told him to find another foreman.

Months later, when I was working in Manchester, I met Whipple's secretary, a nice girl called Mary Pagan. When I worked at Kemps, I was too shy to speak to her. Now I bumped into her at Leeds station and took her to a cafe for tea. She said I had been a terrible snob when I was their works foreman. I am still trying to figure that one out. I was pretty well frightened of the whole set-up. Anyway, that was the last I saw of Mary. We parted good friends; I would have liked to have known her better.

Kemps printed and published trade directories and local Chamber of Commerce directories, a straight crib of Kelly's Directories. They had teams of salesmen, on commission, selling space to unsuspecting shopkeepers and small traders. The rate was £20 for a full page advertisement down to £1 for a small entry. The big directories contained 4,000 pages. I marked up the ad-copy each morning for setting on three linotype machines. A night shift set the directory entries on the same machines. There would be at least 2,000 pages of advertising in each book. Payment was on presentation of proofs. We printed off 100 sheets from each forme and only fifty copies were finally bound, so the real value to advertisers was nil. A few of these fifty finished copies were sent to reference libraries.

Some of the salesmen rumbled the racket and decided to cash in on it. They got jobbing printers to set and proof the advertisements and then went to collect payment from the advertisers. The copy never even got near the Directories and the jobbing printer never got paid. Eventually this was disclosed and the Public

Prosecutor took up the case. By this time, however, I had moved on.

I had taken a day off from Kemps to go for an interview at the *Bury Times* as advert layout man, or designer, as he would now be called. I had been offered the job but was so depressed by the sight of Bury on a wet day that I had followed up another possibility. David Ryder, through his uncle, Fred Blackburn, had found work at the *Daily Mail* in Manchester. It was permanent night work but the pay, in the region of £9, was twice as much as I was getting as a foreman book printer. I called at the *Mail* and asked to see David. He introduced me to the head printer, Tom Phipps, who offered me a holiday relief job on a Ludlow typesetting machine, to start in two months' time. I accepted although I had never seen a Ludlow machine before.

I left Kemps Directories and obtained a month's training at the Ludlow agents, Martin J. Slattery, Bouverie Street, between Fleet Street and the Embankment; next door to *Punch* and the *News of the World*. I got lodgings in Clapham Common and saw nothing of London that I can remember except the short walk from the lodgings to the tube, and from Temple Station to Bouverie Street. At the end of the month, I took up my new job at the *Daily Mail* in Deansgate, Manchester, as a Ludlow expert.

On my first night at the *Mail*, I asked another compositor where a certain type face was kept.

'Fuck off, you!' he answered. 'There's too many Yorkshiremen here already.'

That was in 1933 when there were four hundred unemployed compositors signing the books in Manchester alone. For the next seven years until I was called up for the Army in 1940, I worked a 6 p.m. to 2 a.m. shift, first setting headlines and advertisements on Ludlow machines and, later on, making up pages on the stone – that is, assembling the various components of the page, headlines, pictures, type columns, rules and advertisements, into a composite page of type metal and zinc photo engravings on a flat steel bench. This work was carried out in collaboration with a sub-editor who had to cut or shorten news stories if they were too long for the available space and write headlines with the appropriate number of letters so that when set in a suitable size of type, they would nicely fill the space allowed at the top of each story.

All this was done at great speed. When the page was made-up and locked up into a steel frame, a rough proof was taken for the editor's approval, after which the type pages were moulded and cast into semi-cylindrical, half-dustbin-sized plates, from which the papers were printed.

The place where a national newspaper is produced, whether in Fleet Street, Manchester or Glasgow, as well as containing a highly technical mass-production operation, is also a colourful social organisation. There were some great characters at the *Mail.* Jack Jamieson, our bibulous Father of the Chapel, was the best swearer I have ever known in or out of the barrack room. He usually started with 'Jesus f..... Christ!' and went on to invoke the Pope and the Pope's unmarried parents; venereal diseases of various types were attributed to the objects of his invective; natural functions, personal plumbing and human anatomy filled the gaps in what could be a hundred words of continuous blasphemy without repetition. When he merely wanted to express surprise, and not admonish, he would start with 'Jesus Henry God!'.

I had to report to 'Jammy', as he was affectionately called, on first entering the works before I could make a start. Within an hour, I did not exactly run, but moved rather quickly across the floor.

'Come here, Sidney Wooderson' (then champion sprinter), called out Jamieson. 'We don't run here.'

And it would have been as much as my union card was worth to answer back or question the Chapel discipline.

The head printer, Tom Phipps, was a tiny man with a powerful and penetrating look in his eyes. His successor was Jack Hutchinson, or 'Hell Fire Jack' as we called him, and the chief engineer was a beady-eyed little man who stood peering at us from doorways like a copper's nark. We called him 'The Ferret'.

During my first week at the *Mail*, I was so nervous that instead of going down the room, past the overseer's desk and the other men, to get to the lavatory, I peed into a tin in a dark corner of the composing room and poured it out of the window into Deansgate. The wash-house-cum-lavatory and locker room was a place of noisy argument and horseplay. David Ryder, my very tough mate from Batley, used to strip to the waist to wash the ink and sweat off. If any Lancastrian as much as raised a whisper about interlopers from Leeds, David would challenge the entire swearing, steaming assembly.

'Come on, then, any two of you – outside, or shut your piss-begotten traps.'

Then his uncle, Fred Blackburn, a steady and responsible craftsman, or some other older compositor, would tease David out of his anger with a leg-pull about

Yorkshire's cricket champion, Len Hutton, or Batley rugby team's current hooker. Within minutes, back at work on the stone and under pressure from the clock to get the edition away, the quick up, quick down tempers would give way, first to banter and then to the full, friendly co-operation which the circumtances demanded in order to get the paper to press on time and beat the *Express* to the trains. This was particularly the case if we thought we had a scoop. Newspaper scoops are almost a thing of the past now: television and radio scoop the lot.

The social stratification of printers is sharply defined. Jobbing and book printers felt that they were superior craftsmen, but pay and conditions were so much better in news offices that the newsmen looked down on the jobbing printer. They were both in the same union but had separate divisions. The news men were the more militant and usually won their arguments with management because of the time-critical nature of news. A book is still a book even if it is a day or two late from the press, but when a newspaper misses the train to its distribution centre, it is only fit for pulping.

Jobbing printers, on the other hand, always felt themselves to be rather an oppressed class. If they protested too much about hours, holidays and pay, they could find themselves out of a job very easily and for a long time, too. This was the situation from 1840 to 1940. Whenever the printing unions challenged the employers to a showdown and took a strike ballot, it was always said to be the jobbers who let the side down by voting against strike action.

The head proof reader at the *Mail* was always a graduate and his reading staff kept themselves a little apart. Linotype operators were white collar workers, at the top of the wages bracket. Stone hands or makers-up earned a special responsibility bonus working directly with the sub-editors and always against the clock. Their job ranked above the linotype operators. David was the fastest maker-up I have ever seen and the most reliable when time was running out. I prided myself on being able to help out any junior sub-editor who was stuck for a headline or crosshead, and sometimes took the initiative by cutting a story to fit if the sub-editor was too busy. This was usually done by holding off the last paragraph of a story, knocking off enough sentences until the metal would fit the column, and then putting back the last paragraph, provided the story ending still made sense – a practice which got me into trouble with the leader page sub more than once.

During those seven pre-war years, I had no great ambition but I did continue my part-time studies, without much purpose or persistence. I had short bursts of lessons in German from Mrs.Langford, widow of a celebrated *Guardian* music critic, Sam Langford. I took singing lessons but my light tenor voice never really developed and I got stuck on drawing-room ballads. I entered a few music festival singing competitions in the North and usually came in fourth. I then signed on for a Ruskin College correspondence course on English Literature, wrote essays and some stiff sonnets but discontinued the course when the fine weather came. I had the urge to be better educated but not the application: as my school reports invariably stated: 'Could do much better but plays too much'.

At twenty-five, I still had no experience of physical love and was shy in female company. As Jack Jamieson said: 'I bet if he saw it, he'd throw his cap at it.' Then in one year, I proposed three times to different girls whom I scarcely knew and propositioned several hostesses at the local dance hall, but always at impossible moments. I was briefly engaged to a charming girl and then panicked and bailed out, which was a pity – but that's life. My older sister who helped in my upbringing had just died under tragic circumstances and I was deeply upset. This had much to do with breaking off the engagement. I felt lost and was too immature to risk a vow.

* * *

In the summer of 1939, an old friend from Harrogate, George Woods, who kept a splendid Irish linen shop in Station Parade, wrote to say that he was going walking in Switzerland and would I care to join him? The idea appealed to me greatly and after an exchange of letters about routes and costs, we set off from Waterloo Station, heading for Kandersteg in the Oberland. We took a sleeper from Paris and at breakfast in the dining-car, we sat with two charming and cheerful girls, Norah and Betty. By way of introduction, we shared the two remaining bread rolls among the four of us until a fresh supply came. They were going beyond Kandersteg to the Loetschental Valley to start a walking tour.

When we arrived at Kandersteg, there was a cloud ceiling just above chimney height. Crocodiles of rain-coated tourists trailed up from the station to the hotels. George suggested we got the next train down the line and went to the Loetschental where we might find our two attractive breakfast companions. After asking at about a dozen hotels along five miles of the Valley road, we eventually saw the girls in the lounge of a small hotel at Kippel. We registered theatrical surprise and remarked on the pleasant coincidence of our coming to the same place!

A brief account of what followed is that we teamed up for a delightful holiday and by the time we were back at work, Betty and I were showing all the signs of being seriously in love. We were intending to get married by Christmas but her parents urged a small delay. Impatiently, we waited a few more months and on May 4th, 1940, we were married in Sussex, at St. Phillip's Church, Burwash Common. It was a great day and we departed very happily for our honeymoon in the Lake District.

The war against Hitler's Germany had started. I remember walking with Betty down Dentdale one weekend and hearing the solemn voices of BBC news announcers on farmhouse radios, reporting the fate of France. At each village we went through the news was more devastating. Britain had declared war on September 3rd, 1939, and first there was the phony war, followed only too soon by the great blitz attacks on London.

Before the war I had tried to join the Territorial Army, not out of any sense of military zeal but because, like my eldest brother Henry in 1917, it seemed to be the right thing to do. I found that they didn't have territorial training in the afternoons for night workers, so when conscription started, I waited until my number came up which it duly did in August 1940. At this time, I was still working for the *Daily Mail* and living with Betty in Withington. We had been married only a few months. It was a bitter blow to be separated so soon but much worse for Betty at home than for me, busy as I was with an entirely new world of people and experiences.

The most remarkable thing about the first year in the

army was the way in which millions of individuals, each with his own ego to nurse and his own eccentricities to be accommodated, were knocked into some sort of conformity by means of square bashing and the rough tongue of an NCO. Within a month, we were all behaving like animals in a circus: jumping to attention at the sight of an officer, banging down our heels until our cartilages got frayed at the edges and slapping our rifles with such force, in a vain attempt to please the drill sergeant, that our fingers stung in a way that reminded me of Dingy Horner's cane at school, twenty years earlier.

In a very short time, one part of our personalities became a responding unit, like a Pavlovian puppy, while the other part, according to intelligence and strength of character, retained, and even developed, its obstinate individuality. The two sides looked at each other like a man in a barber's chair looks on while his image in the mirror is manipulated to suit the hand with the scissors. For the good soldier, sufficient unto the day were the fatigues and frustrations thereof. Those men who looked back with remorse or forward with fear seldom survived in a sane condition – in fact, seldom survived.

Most of the time I was able to get on with what each day demanded of me, either willingly and cheerfully, or in a state of brainwashed passivity. And most of the time I enjoyed barrack room life with all its stupid routine and coarse vulgarity. Weekend leave was a great delight when Betty would come up to Catterick and we would stay at some small hotel in the district. This was before we acquired our house at 70 Frenchgate, Richmond. At camp, I did four weeks' basic training which consisted largely of drill on the barrack square and physical training in the gymnasium. At the end of this period, most of us knew how to march and turn in some semblance of order, and how to hold a rifle. We defended the garrison area with wooden staves as there were not enough rifles to go round, against the invader that never came. Such was the state of the armed preparedness of Britain in 1940.

We lived twenty men to a hut. The huts were built for the 1914 war and most of the time, when we were not marching or learning the parts of a bren gun, was spent spreading Johnson's wax polish in a thick layer on the rough floor, trying to bring some sort of surface to it with a bumper, which was a heavy iron plate lined with felt and hinged to a long pole.

We were a very mixed bunch in B Squadron of the 51st Training Regiment. Our reactions to military training and discipline must have followed a fairly predictable bell curve pattern. Most people fitted in fairly well, give or take a few punishment drills for late on parade or dumb insolence. A few were very quick to adapt and appeared to be born soldiers; one or two could just never make it. It was not a matter of intelligence or lack of it, unless the real test of intelligence is whether or not one can bend and survive.

My pre-war friend, Walter Briggs, starved himself ill rather than stomach the food which the rest of us thrived on. His reaction to Depot life was the same as that of T.E. Lawrence in 1922 when he wrote these opening words in *The Mint*: 'God, this is awful'.

Johnny Yorke, a pale intellectual with hair parted down the middle, couldn't drill, couldn't shoot, and was totally uncoordinated. He had Bloomsbury friends on the political left which caused him no end of trouble. He was constantly being sent for by the CO to account for his movements and his mail was opened by Security. He was quite innocent but this surveillance made him sick with worry. Once, he and I had an unauthorised night out at the King's Head in Richmond, with our wives, which we could sometimes arrange by modestly bribing the guard sergeant, Shady Lane. It was vital that we should be back in barracks before roll-call at 6 a.m. On this particular occasion when we tried to leave the King's Head at 5.45, all the doors were locked, there was no night porter and the keys could not be found. We were securely locked in. The windows did not want to open and in any case, the last thing we needed was to be seen climbing out of an hotel window in the early hours by a prowling red cap. Eventually we forced a back window and got back to camp just in time to avoid arrest.

I was arrested only once at Catterick – for 'having a woman in men's quarters'. Betty was 'camp following' and we were going out to a dance. She was due to meet me out of barracks and as it was raining, came in while I changed my boots. This suspicious behaviour brought two red caps at the double and they didn't care for my explanation. So I was hauled up in front of Major Richardson. The dipso-major gave me a mild ticking-off, but when he happened to see Betty on a Richmond bus a week later, he came across and said to her: 'Woman, you should know better than hanging around camp getting my men into trouble'. At that moment, Betty, pregnant with our first child, thought that life was most unfair.

Major Richardson was one of the extraordinary characters that made an otherwise dull establishment like Catterick Camp into a theatre in which could be observed the bizarre tricks God has played in the creation of some of his creatures. I got to know 'Ritchie' quite well but I doubt if, through his semi-permanent alcoholic glaze, he ever saw me clearly enough to know me.

His wife was an Alsatian – that is, a lady from Alsace. Richardson must have been in his early fifties, but looked older; tall, thin and bloodshot. What his regimental background was I have no idea but, at Catterick, he was in charge of the RAC Wireless Wing, where radio operators were trained for tanks and armoured cars.

I volunteered to be his batman for a week to let his own man take his Christmas leave. On the first morning, I boiled the eggs for twenty-five minutes because the electric ring wouldn't raise enough turbulence in the egg pan to prove that the water was boiling. I took the breakfast tray into the bedroom. The Major and his lady were sitting up in bed reading Agatha Christies, and drinking hard. He had three empty beer bottles by his side and his wife was half way down what had been, half an hour earlier, an unopened bottle of sherry. It looked like Act 3, Scene 1 of a Feydeau farce. An hour later I went to collect the tray. The very hard-boiled eggs were cracked but untouched.

'Partridge,' said the Major, 'do you think you could try poaching the eggs tomorrow?'

James Scot was another colleague at Catterick, a young aesthete with a passion for T.E. Lawrence. Jim came down to Bovington as a tank driving instructor and got to know Sgt. Knowles and his wife, who looked after Lawrence's cottage at Cloud's Hill. The Knowles were kind to Jim, allowing him to read Lawrence's books and rest on his 'Meum', the square oxhide-covered divan. Then one day, Jim was gone, posted, of course, to Arabia where he did the Damascus Road bit. After the war, he came home to write his magnum opus which he set out to do in a disused coastguard shelter at Abbotsbury behind Chesil Beach. He lived rough and wrote intermittently until his tea chest was full of verse and prose fragments.

Jim had had college training in horticulture. When the literary genius failed to emerge, he got a job as a gardener at a ladies' college near Herne Hill. He always had a fair turn of speed as a cyclist and at Catterick Camp had ridden with Reg Harris who was to become British and Olympic sprint cycling champion. Jim got back into the cycling game at the Herne Hill track and after some successes, joined a velodrome circus in Valencia, touring Europe and the Argentine in this spectacular but severely bent sport. All the races but one in every meeting were pre-cooked so that first the local champion would win, then there would be a crash followed by a fight on the track, then the baddy would win a race to the shrieks and boos of the crowd. There was always one open race so that the professionals had some measure of their relative performances. Jim raced his way round the world for seven years and then came back to Dorset for a short holiday, and stayed forever.

Early on in Catterick, I decided that the only civilised unit fit to work in was the Wireless Wing. Being a driver-mechanic was a cold and dirty job in winter and the gunnery school was full of aggressive NCO's who scared the life out of me. So I worked my way on to the staff of the Wireless Wing by doing reasonably well in the exams and apparently impressing the Major as a lecturer. The fact was, and still is, that I enjoy having an audience and can usually get a fair response. Our level of radio teaching was not technically too demanding. For the first courses, I used to read up the Admiralty *Handbook of Wireless* which was more advanced than our standard. This usually enabled me to deal with the inevitable clever dicks who had done physics at university. But if they asked questions I couldn't deal with, I never found it embarrassing to ask one of the graduates to come and explain the problem to the class. I read up new matter the night before and lectured on it confidently the next day.

Some of the Highland Light Infantry troopers were a bit hard to teach but I would have been glad to have them alongside me in any battle situation, whether or not they knew which way the electrons flowed through a triode-pentode. On one officer course, I had an Etonian lieutenant who had the greatest difficulty with the morse code. Most students reached twelve words a minute without much trouble in six weeks. This character couldn't put any words together at all. I asked if he could tell me what the core of the difficulty was.

'I'm fff-frightfully sorry,' he replied, 'But I ccc-can't tell the d-dots from the dd-dashes.'

My year as a teacher in the Wireless Wing was one of the most satisfying experiences I can remember. I saw Betty often enough not to feel totally cut off, I was learning new things all the time and getting satisfaction from a higher-than-average pass rate for my students. Between lectures some of us on the staff played chess without a chess set. We chalked squares and pieces on the blackboard and made the moves with a duster. Major Richardson was bowler-hatted just before I left Catterick.

Introducing his successor to the Wireless Wing staff at a sad little farewell ceremony, he looked at the man and then at the ceiling and his melancholy parting words were, 'How are the mighty fallen.'

When it began to look as if I would be on the Wireless Wing staff for at least a few months, we rented a small cottage on The Green under Richmond Castle walls, beside the River Swale. We had our friends from the camp in for tea and whatever food we could raise in sufficient quantities. There was Jack Barker, a Pennine farmer, who taught us the whistles he used to control his sheep dogs on the hills, Iky Freedman from Blackpool and a tough Liverpudlian, Alan Poynton, who was, of all improbable occupations for a man of his build, a ladies' hat salesman.

In 1941 I was posted to the tank school at Bovington in Dorset as a sergeant instructor. Bovington Camp is in Thomas Hardy country, a vast area of sandy scrubland which, in Hardy's great novel *Tess of the D'Urbevilles* is known to the D'Urbevilles as Egdon Heath. 'Tess' is courted beside the Stour which runs between the camp and the Seven Stars pub on the Wool-Dorchester road. The wonder is that half of the Royal Armoured Corps soldiers were not drowned in this deceptively deep river as they staggered back to barracks at closing time over the flimsy wooden bridges.

'The camp is beautifully put,' wrote T.E. Lawrence to A.E. Chambers when, under the name T.E. Shaw, he joined the Royal Tank Corps at Bovington Camp in March, 1923. 'A wide heath of flint and sand with pines and oak trees, and much rhododendron coming slowly into bloom. When the heather flowers in a few weeks there will be enough to please me.'

The tank school had been there since the First World War and still flourishes, having trained new generations to win the last war. On a straight stretch of the undulating road which runs north and south through the camp, Lawrence – scholar-soldier and disillusioned leader of an Arab revolt – killed himself in 1935, crashing his Brough Superior motorcycle in a swerve to avoid two boys on bicycles.

At Bovington we taught a slightly more advanced level of wireless operating and radio theory to groups of officers and NCO's. One of my students was a Sgt. Ivan Makarov from the Calgary Regiment of the Canadian Armoured Corps. Ivan was unbelievably Russian: stockily built with powerful shoulders and an operatic bass voice. He was a gentle, generous trooper when sober but uncontrollable when drunk. At reveille, he used to reach under his bed for a tin of canned heat (jellified meths.) which he spooned shakily into his mouth, when he could find it – his mouth, that is – with the tarnished tea spoon rattling against his gold-plated teeth like castanets in a bolero. Another student, Captain Reddyhough, owner of a West Riding mill, gave me a pound for coaching him through his exams; all highly contrary to the spirit and letter of King's Regulations but a kind thought and useful at the time.

For practical training, we went swanning around Dorset in armoured cars or jeeps, keeping in touch with each other and with base by radio. The favourite rendezvous was the bakehouse in Moreton, famous at that time for its doughnuts. Sgt. Kearsley, a Geordie who taught me to sing 'The Lampton Worm', once ate twenty-eight doughnuts for his elevenses, thus eclipsing Sgt. Wolkind's previous best performance of a round two dozen. Wolkind, familiarly known as Spring-Heeled

Jack on account of his bouncing walk, became Town Clerk of Tower Hamlets. I saw the back of his bouncy step going down Fetter Lane in 1975 and immediately recognised it, but he disappeared into the Fleet Street traffic before I could touch him on the shoulder. A year later I noticed his name in the paper in connection with some housing problem in Tower Hamlets, and gave him a ring. We met for lunch at the Waldorf but, alas, no doughnuts were served!

Captain Adam Maitland, a kilted Scot, wrote good reports on my radio teaching and Captain Parsons who was OC my department, suggested that I should apply for a commission. With false modesty, rather like a small boy declining a tip from his uncle until pressed, I suggested that officer rank was not for me, and five minutes later was persuaded that I was just the sort of chap they needed.

I went before a War Office Selection Board at Winchester where I remember giving a ten-minute lecture on a subject picked out of a hat, getting a tree trunk over a stream with the help of four other contestants and putting a lawn mower together from a heap of bits on a table. The selection process took three days all told and my room mate was a large shambling Welshman who knew a lot about Winchester Cathedral and kept his pyjamas in a brown paper parcel under his bed because he said he slept more comfortably in the raw. This was Frank Owen, ex-secretary to Lloyd George, Liberal MP, PR man to Mountbatten in South East Asia, editor of the *Evening Standard* in 1940 and of the *Daily Mail* after the war, 1947-50.

Owen was turned forty when he was called up into

the Army. A question was asked in the House of Commons about him and Cassandra of the *Daily Mirror*: why had these two distinguished London journalists who were doing such a useful job helping to keep up morale in blitzed London, been called up in middle age for military service?

Ernest Bevin, then Minister of Labour and National Service, answered the question in his characteristically elephantine way: 'They are more use to me in the Army.' In previous weeks, the press had been critical of Bevin's decision to call up women for war work. After only a few weeks at Sandhurst, Owen was hauled away first to write a war diary for a general, and then to serve Mountbatten in the field of communications, taking my gunnery notes, which he had borrowed, with him. His quick commission led to another question in the House: 'Why has Trooper Owen, RAC, been commissioned to the rank of major after only ten weeks at OCTU – who is pulling the strings?'

6

Sandhurst and the Eighth Army

So far as I could tell at the time, the purpose of Sandhurst was to see if the staff could break you physically and mentally. It was by far the most testing time of the war for me. The discipline was extreme and I didn't take to it kindly. We had hours of drill on the 'square' in front of the main building. The technical training was easier than the courses I had taught at Bovington: physical training and the Battle School in Snowdonia were tough on the youngsters though less so for the older cadets who were not as quick but had more stamina.

We 'attacked' the buildings on top of Snowdon with bren guns and two-inch mortars, and I was put on several charges when we got back for not conserving the unexpired portion of the day's ration. This resulted in a week of sadistic punishment drill and, what was harder to take, a strict ticking-off from a cretinous captain. In the end, I got through to the passing-out parade and was commissioned as a lieutenant in the Inns of Court Regiment, an armoured car unit in training near Newcastle-upon-Tyne. I don't think I can have shone as a regimental officer. My squadron leader said I had a tendency to be too familiar with the troops, which, come to think of it, was what R.D. Whipple of Kemps Directories had said when I was his works manager: 'Too familiar with the men, Partridge, that's your trouble.'

Early in December 1943, I was posted to an Eighth Army holding unit in North Africa which was there to replace some of the heavy casualties suffered by units in Sicily and Italy.

We landed in Algiers on Christmas Day, 1943, after a dreary journey in convoy by way of Greenland and Newfoundland, a route which must have been chosen to confuse the enemy: it certainly had no other redeeming feature.

We moved from Algiers to El Guerar some way inland and eastwards. This was a tented camp on high ground and, by God, it was cold at nights. We plodded around in snow and mud trying to keep warm and stave off boredom. I was now thirty-two which was considered to be too ripe an age for a lieutenant to be a tank troop leader and so, in March, when the weather improved, I was given thirty men and a sergeant, all either ex-hospital cases or new out from England, to train and deliver to various regiments now engaged in the battle for Rome.

I took this scratch team to Philipville where we camped on the beach awaiting a convoy to Naples. We waited for a couple of weeks during which time, by using a blend of methods employed by a Butlin's holiday camp and an approved school, I managed to produce a cheerful, healthy unit which was later reported by a major in Italy to be the brightest shower of reinforcements he had had since the campaign started. We crossed to Naples and after a night in a transit camp, set off again in trucks to Bovino, a location south of Foggia and east of the hilltop town of Benevento where they make a very drinkable gin.

The history of the campaign in Italy was written up by

Eric Linklater and published by HMSO in 1951. I met Linklater several times when he came to stay at the Eighth Army headquarters to compile his notes for the official history.

My own part in this six-hundred day series of battles was totally unremarkable. All I can say is that I was there and glad to be so, even as a junior scene-shifter on that enormous stage. I arrived during the long drawn-out battle for Monte Cassino but knew nothing of the fighting except for the almost continuous rumble of bombing and shelling in the distance. The Cassino battle went on from January 29th to May 18th, 1944. The extraordinary thing was how little the average soldier or officer knew about events outside his own immediate area. We were only a few miles south of the fighting but encapsulated in our own little world.

I took over a set of buildings which included a small schoolhouse and offices arranged around a large courtyard, once an administrative centre for a wide agricultural community in one of Mussolini's more enlightened efforts to improve the lot of the southern peasant. After we left it, the place was turned into another large holding and training centre. It was surrounded by malarial marshes but had been selected by a colonel at HQ and allocated to our use because it contained one of the few bathrooms in rural Southern Italy. We divided our working days between training and malaria control.

Training consisted of cross-country runs and improvised assault courses with shooting practice when I could scrounge enough ammunition. The anti-malarial exercise was the draining of marshes, digging and clearing irrigation ditches and DDT spraying. Between times, we ate and slept and played a lot of football. I got into serious trouble with the quartermaster in Foggia for failing to account for twenty-two pairs of boots of various sizes: I had written these off as worn out to obtain new pairs so as to convert the old ones into football boots with home-made studs. We also managed to get good rations of food, drink and blankets, ostensibly for the entertainment of VIPs en route between Caserta and the east coast who often used us as a staging post.

We were soon joined a by a detachment of Madras Sappers (Indian engineers) under Major Boydell. We lived well, the Indian cooks providing superb dishes out of Army rations, plus a few local eggs, chickens and bottles of wine. Asti was not far away and the famous sweet, bubbly Spumanti came in large quantities in exchange for corned beef. Curry was a speciality, and when we became too popular a calling point for travelling brass hats on account of our gastronomic reputation, an element of selection had to be introduced. Any guest who showed signs of becoming a bore or a nuisance was treated to the cook's 'Inferno' which was a special curry, skilfully served to the unwelcome guest only, while the rest of the table had the normal excellent fare. The cook's 'Special Inferno' was so hot that even the most peppery ex-Poona colonel went puce and broke into a violent sweat as he looked around the table to see how the junior officers were coping with this fiendish concoction. We were all smiles while the hapless visitor gradually lost the roof of his mouth trying not to lose face.

Gradually, my troop was called forward to replace casualties in the regiments; I asked to be posted to a fighting unit but was refused, thank God, because I was too old to be a regimental troop leader and too inexperienced in the field for any more senior appointment, or perhaps for being 'just too familiar with the troops'.

The monastery at Cassino was taken on May 18th, 1944. On the 23rd, Allied troops broke out from Anzio beach-head and the Fifth Army entered Rome on June 4th. On my thirty-third birthday – August 18th – I joined the Eighth Army Headquarters as a liaison officer.

The line of strong defences between Rimini in the east and Pisa in the west was known as the Gothic Line. These formidable defences were in great depth, taking advantage of terrain that was almost unassailable. In the west and centre, mountain range followed mountain range, and in the east, a network of lateral rivers, canals and vineyards reduced visibility almost to zero and made tank going impossible.

Eighth Army HQ had just moved from the Siena area to the east coast in a massive but well-concealed exercise. I had been given the old location map reference to report to and a nervous driver with a clapped-out 15cwt truck in which to get there. Between Siena and Florence, I ran into a VIP convoy and recognised Winston Churchill sitting in the second car, complete with large cigar and raised V fingers. He was there as a decoy (probably the only time he was ever used as a dead duck!) to deceive the enemy into thinking that the main attack would come in the central sector through Florence. The move to the east was top secret and at no military unit in the district could I find out a new Army HQ location map reference. I enquired at one unit and just for asking, was almost arrested by the CO for careless talk. The adjutant of this unit, taking pity and accepting my credentials, said: 'Just keep going east, old boy. You'll find them.'

So I left Siena without regret and moved east, through Arezzo and east again, on minor roads into deep vineyard country. For miles and miles I saw no-one – no allied troops, no farming peasants. Then, approaching Citta de Castello, I heard gunfire and, more ominously, the crack of shells passing overhead. My driver turned even paler than his usual pale self and threatened to bale out. We came down a side road from the west into the main north/south road through the town. At the junction, we stopped to look at the map. The door of a house opened, first an inch or two, and then wide, and a woman emerged with a bunch of flowers, taken from a vase in the window, which she threw into our ancient truck. I asked in my very limited Italian:

'Dove soldati Inglesi?' ('Where are the English soldiers?')

'Ne-enti soldati Inglesi,' she replied. 'Tedeski soldati la . . .' ('There are no English soldiers – German soldiers are there . . .') and she pointed round the corner to the left.

Driver White didn't need a second bidding to turn right at the corner, and we belted off south as fast as the terrible truck would take us. There may have been shorter routes to the east but we went south for forty miles, passing Assissi on the hills to our left, with never a second thought for St. Francis or the birds. At Foligno, we turned left and north-east towards Ancona and on this new main road, joined an apparently endless convoy of tanks and heavy artillery which was moving towards the Adriatic coast. From one of these units, I obtained the location of Main HQ Eighth Army which was now at Jesi, ten miles from the coast and ten miles west of Ancona. Before dusk, I reported to Brigadier Ivor Moore in his caravan in a wood.

'Glad to have you,' he said. 'Have good reports, but there's no promotion here, young man.'

'So long as there's a job to do,' I replied, 'I'll be content.'

Apparently this was the right thing to say to Ivor, a kindly man who stood for no bullshit. Next day, I was briefed and sent off to reconnoitre the various approach routes to the Gothic Line.

Meanwhile, at home, Betty was living at 70 Frenchgate, Richmond, near Catterick camp in Yorkshire, in the tall terraced house overlooking the River Swale. By now we had two baby girls: Judith, born in April 1942 and Ruth, born thirteen months later. Sadly, I scarcely got to know them in babyhood. I was overseas during their three most formative years.

Letters to and from home were frequent and loving. Looking back more than forty years to my Army days, I remember the fun, the comradeship and the excitement. But Betty reminds me of the miserable letters I wrote describing the December convoy to North Africa in 1943 which was routed via Iceland; of the bitterly cold winter we endured under canvas in the Algerian hills, and the knee-deep mud in which we wallowed during the wretched 1944 autumn on the Adriatic coastal plain. Fortunately, one tends to forget those unhappy times, and to remember one's Army days as a time of travel and opportunity, filled with new experiences, fresh faces and many warm friendships.

During the time at Jesi, General Oliver Leese was Commander of the Eighth Army. Both British and French troops were being withdrawn from the Mediterranean theatre to strengthen the armies in northern Europe and in the south of France. General Alexander, commanding all the Mediterranean and Middle East forces, planned a concerted attack by the Fifth and Eighth armies which were to move parallel up Italy from a line north of Rome. Oliver Leese disliked the idea of having two competing armies, one of which was almost certain to have the easier going and so run ahead of the other. He claimed this would be bad for morale. Alexander acceded to Leese's new plan for two coordinated but separate attacks: the Fifth Army going up through the central Apennines and the Eighth Army up the eastern ridges and coastal plain.

These two polyglot armies included regiments of Poles, Canadians, Americans, Indians, Irish, South Africans, British and Partisan brigades. The Gothic Line battles started with an attack by the 4th Indian Division on August 25th, 1944.

One of my tasks as a liaison officer at Eighth Army HQ was to visit combatant units on the Eighth Army line and report back to the brigadier in charge of Armoured Fighting Vehicles (AFV) on certain aspects of the situation which could not be, or at least, were not, included in official reports. This might be for security reasons or, in certain cases where troop morale had hit a very low spot, a matter of discretion. At one time, desertions from an infantry brigade which had been in action, without home leave, for more than three years were so frequent that the CO stopped arraigning deserters before a court martial. He would let the troop decide if they wanted the soldier back and, if they did, the offence was overlooked and no report made to any higher authority.

My visits to units in the line were sometimes resented

and sometimes welcomed with warm hospitality. At first the arrival of someone from the 'Army' was treated with surprise and suspicion. Gradually I got on personal terms with brigade majors, COs and their adjutants, bringing information that was useful to them, as well as asking my questions. 'What's the score?' was a typical opening gambit on either side. Troops in forward positions very seldom knew what was happening on their flanks. On more than one occasion shots were exchanged between two of our own units, emerging from mist in the early morning on either side of a hill feature.

It is all a long time ago, but I can remember many incidents in vivid detail as if they were recorded on video tapes. My 'most embarrassing moment', to quote a once-popular radio programme, was when I gave the Brigade Major of 25th Armoured Brigade, information that had been doing the rounds at Army HQ for weeks, that one of his units, 142 Reconnaissance Regiment, was to be disbanded. The break-up of a regiment is an emotional event at any time: in wartime, it can be traumatic. When I returned to Army HQ, Brigadier Moore was waiting on his caravan steps at the entrance to our camp. He beckoned me over.

'Where have you been?' he asked.

'25th Armoured Brigade,' I replied.

'Who did you see?'

'The Brigade Major.'

'What did you say?'

I told Moore that I had said one of the 25th Armoured units might be for the chop.

'You may like to know,' said Moore, 'that the Army Commander was going to release that information to them in a special staff conference tomorrow. Don't ever do that again!'

'No, sir,' I replied smartly, and that was the last I heard of it. My well intentioned but indiscreet 'leak' had been signalled to him as I was on my way back from the Brigade.

I was once ordered off the road by General (Ginger) Hawkesworth, the commander of 46th Division, because he said my Daimler scout car was in the way of his attacking force. He had, in fact, ordered all vehicles off the road except 138th Brigade so that he could make a quick advance from San Clemente to Coriano. German opposition here was very strong and the 46th Division was brought to a halt a mile from Coriano, in front of Croce. This was extremely difficult terrain for tanks and heavy armour. Ridge after mountain ridge was fiercely defended.

To the west, the Fifth Army was making rapid progress in pursuit of an enemy which, although offering dogged resistance, was already showing signs of defeat. Milan, Turin and other towns north of the Lombardy Plain were now in the hands of Partisans, while on the Adriatic side, swinging around Lake Commaccio, Eighth Army divisions hammered the German Panzer and Parachute regiments into a desperate retreat. Then, with the New Zealand Armoured Brigade leading, the race was on to reach Trieste before Tito's Partisans totally occupied the town. Already as German troops withdrew, local hotel employees were popping Partisan flags out of the bedroom windows and claiming that they had defeated the Germans and captured the city.

By May 2nd, 1945, the New Zealanders were in Trieste where General Freyberg took the surrender of the German forces who had been trying, in the last phase of the war, to deny to the Russian-supported Yugoslav Fourth Army, this important access to the sea.

I went to Trieste a few days later to report on the situation for the AFV section of Army HQ, then at Mestre. Remarkable though it may seem, I took with me carrier pigeons from the Royal Corps of Signals' loft which accompanied us all the way up Italy. It took the handlers only a few days to home the birds at each new location as we moved up country. The lofts were placed at the site and the birds kept in without food for 24 hours; then they were released with food in their boxes. They flew three times around the site and returned for a feed. This procedure was repeated for a few days with the birds being taken in baskets a bit farther away each time. Within a week, you could take them fifty miles and they would return safely at an average speed of about forty m.p.h. The pigeons were back from Trieste to Mestre, across the Adriatic – long before I could have made it by road against the tidal wave of Eighth Army transport moving in the opposite direction – with a short message on cigarette paper in a capsule attached to a leg.

Trieste became a political prize among the Allies as well as a vital military target. Tito was desperate to take the town and its surrounding territory, Venezia Giulia, which stretched from the Austrian border, including the Istrian Peninsula, and what became, from 1947 to 1954, the Free Territory of Trieste before it was added to Italy.

It was the wisdom and foresight of General Alexander that persuaded Churchill not to press for the occupation of the whole of Venezia Giulia but to support Italy's claim for a stable eastern boundary including Trieste. Alexander was strongly opposed to the idea of having to commit Eighth Army troops in battle against their former allies, the Yugoslav Partisans, for whom they had developed a considerable respect.

Negotiations over the cease-fire line and the eventual border between Italy and Yugoslavia were intense; both sides, of course, wanted to control 'the high ground'. As I recall, from almost fifty years ago, Brigadier Harry Floyd, the Eighth Army Chief of Staff, sat down with Tito's Chiefs of Staff for a very long meeting. At first, the opposition was intense, then gradually the Slavs were worn down by Floyd's consummate skill as a dealer (I believe he was Chairman of Christie's at some point) and possibly his ability to carry his liquor and keep a cool head. He described the proceedings at a staff meeting which I attended as being 'a bit like buying a carpet from an Egyptian dealer.'

For a graphic and detailed account of this final military and political phase of the Italian campaign, one should read *The Race for Trieste* by Sir Geoffrey Cox (Kimber and Co. 1977). In this revised edition, Sir Geoffrey points out that the struggle for Trieste was 'the first confrontation of the Cold War.' If the Yugoslavs, backed by Russia, had gained Venezia Giulia, it would not have been long before they would have had Austria within their sights. In the event, Russia was not fully prepared to back Tito, hence the eventual split between the two countries.

Harry S. Truman, the new American president, had quickly given his full support to Alexander's strategy and the tactics of moving swiftly to occupy Trieste at the same time as avoiding a war with Tito over the border. Political expediency was placed before military caution; lines of communication and supply were stretched to their limits. In the end, the defeat of the Germans in northern Italy and the occupation of Trieste represented both a great military victory and a massive logistic achievement for the Fifth and Eighth Armies' Service Corps.

The Italian campaign had ended with the spectacular offensive by the Fifth Army through the mountains west of Bologna and a rapid advance by the Eighth Army through the Argenta gap, across the Po Valley and on to Trieste. On May 2nd, 1945, General von Vietinghoff signed the German army's unconditional surrender at Caserta.

It was about a year before I could be released and return home. This was a long, frustrating period for me, but much worse for Betty in Richmond, taking care of Judith and Ruth, struggling with food shortages and rationing. I was stationed at Klagenfurt in Carinthia, that delightful Austrian district full of lakes and mountains near the Yugoslav border.

We were the occupying force and our staff work at Eighth Army HQ was mainly concerned with setting up some sort of civil administration and planning the disbandment of fighting units in southern Europe. I deduced that the plan was to release the armed forces as slowly as possible in order to prevent an upsurge of unemployment at home.

Facilities for sport and recreation were quickly set up as a small reward for a long war. The armoured (ex-cavalry) regiments soon had race meetings organised; we skied every weekend throughout the winter and sailed on Worthersee in the Spring.

In the early mornings, cavalry major, Michael Bell, and I rode our horses through the mountain villages, raising our hats to women in cottage bedrooms as we passed. We had hundreds of horses to choose from and Hungarian colonels for grooms. The horses were captured from German support troops.

I spent three months attending a course in agriculture at the Austrian State Farm School near Spittal in the Drau Valley. My idea was to go into farming when I returned home. Betty had other plans, so we compromised — I scrapped the idea and remained a printer.

The course was very good. We milked and ploughed, learning soil chemistry as well as veterinary and plant biology. It was here at Spittal that I heard the dramatic story of courage and survival involving a Hungarian family, the Mihalyis.

The family consisted of Grandpa and Grandma, both in their sixties, two daughters, two grandchildren and Elizabeth Mihalyi, widow of a Hungarian diplomat. They had arrived in the Drau Valley as refugees with a carriage drawn by a pair of matched grey horses. The carriage was the sole survivor of six vehicles with which they had left the thousand hectare family estate in Hungary when the Russian army arrived from the east. They had packed their more valuable possessions in the carriages, carts and wagons, burying the family silver against the day when they could come back to recover it, and with the entire village, had set off towards the west. As night fell on the first evening, the butler slipped away with the last wagon of the convoy and went back to dig up the buried plate. Then the Russian advance troops caught up with the slower-moving vehicles and plundered them, others being pillaged a few days later by German troops retreating from Yugoslavia and north Italy.

Finally they reached the Drau Valley with the one

carriage and two horses, a few bits of personal jewellery and abundant courage. The family refused to go into the vast Displaced Persons camp which had been set up west of Villach. It was from this camp that refugees were returned to Yugoslavia and Russia to almost certain execution. This had to be done, apparently, to honour a clause on repatriation in the Yalta Agreement between Churchill and Stalin.

Forty years after the event, Count Nikolas Tolstoy and Nigel Watts issued a pamphlet in which they accused Lord Aldington of 'war crimes' and responsibility for sending 70,000 Cossacks and anti-Tito Yugoslavs to their deaths in 1945 when he was Brigadier Toby Lowe with the Eighth Army. Those of us who were serving in this part of Austria at the time were aware from gossip that something very unsavoury was happening. There were reports of mothers jumping with their babies into the River Drau rather than face life behind the Iron Curtain, and of men being shot by guards for refusing to climb into the railway trucks.

It was a human tragedy with causes deep in the politics of war. The fear was that with the war over, Stalin might try to occupy Austria in which case these several hundred thousand 'White Russians' and Slavs would be an acute embarrassment.

Instead of joining the camp when they arrived, the Mihalyis got the use of a barn at Lendorf, in Karnten, and took casual jobs around the local farms, cutting and hauling timber. The grandparents soon made the barn into a home and Elizabeth started to piece together a plan which included getting her two sons, prisoners in Russia, out via the black market and the whole family then emigrating to America. At that time, prisoners in

Russia and Hungary could be bought out to return home if they could provide the money to bribe enough officials along a very devious route.

In a letter she wrote to me from Lendorf in 1949, Elizabeth Mihalyi said:

> 'My mother is 81 and not as strong as she was, living all alone in Hungary, selling a piece of furniture now and then and eating up the price of it, poor darling. But she asks me not to return but go as far away as I can.
>
> 'And now comes my great, great good news!!! You know I have three darling big sons! My second, Louis, 25 years old was released from Russian captivity last July. He came out to Austria 'black' (via the black market), in August. He worked until April gaining his health and strength and then left for Canada. He is working on a farm near Listowel, Ontario.
>
> 'My youngest son, Tommy, worked awful hard on a few acres of land in Hungary for the last three years, but as he does not want to join the Communist Party, they found a reason to put him in prison and illtreat him for two months last autumn. His eldest brother, Andrew, managed to sell rings for 5000 gulden with which he was able to buy his brother free. In Hungary you can buy freedom for people for money; this is a business for communists only; but the freedom only lasts for a few weeks then they put you in prison again. They decided to leave Hungary and come over 'black' to me. Tommy managed to get over after 8 days in the forest hiding. Andrew was also hiding and looking for his brother, trying to find out if they had caught him again. Then he went to friends in Budapest as he

could not go to his own home as the communists would have arrested him in place of Tommy. Then the frost and snow were so bad he waited for a better time to try to get across. The border is so heavily guarded and locked up with wire that people only manage to come over with the help of 2/3000 gulden and as we have no money, I can't help him. But we can at last exchange letters. You see how happy I can be with two of my darlings safe and only one in the hands of the communists. I hope God will guard him and keep him safe. Greetings to you and your dear wife, Yours Sincerely, Elizabeth Mihalyi.'

The little boy and girl at Lendorf were about eight or nine years old. The boy was taken ill and I helped to have him admitted to Klagenfurt Hospital. He was soon cured and returned to the family barn. One of the hospital doctors turned out to be a Hungarian who had connections with the black market traffic in prisoners from Russia, so he was deeply involved in Andrew's escape from prison in Tiflis in the Kaukasus.

With another liaison officer, a New Zealander called Bonny Ross, who had a fine baritone voice, I used to go to the barn from farm school in the evenings for a meal. We usually took large chunks of bully beef, some coffee and a bottle of Cognac. Our hosts provided bread, potatoes and, as an occasional delicacy, bone marrow served like caviar for an hors d'oeuvre. These family meals always started with grace, said by the old man, sitting on his box at the head of the trestle table. The younger women and the two children spoke English; they translated for us and the grandparents. As the meal ended in the unwindowed, candlelit barn, and coffee and cognac were circulated, they would quietly start singing Hungarian folk songs and operatic arias. We joined in the familiar ones. Ross and I sang English folk songs. The singing and talking went on for hours until Grandpa signalled that it was time for everyone to bed down which, as there was only the one room, meant it was time for the guests to depart.

The story of Elizabeth Mihalyi is one of tremendous courage, spiritual resources and optimism. She stayed in Austria until two of her sons got out of Russia and Hungary and settled in America. The eldest son failed in several attempts to come over the wire, married and settled in Budapest. Elizabeth then followed her sons to America and lived in California where she became a well-known portrait painter, equestrian artist and sponsor of the Penninsula Symphony Orchestra. She died in 1986 at the age of 84.

In the great 1939–1945 military drama, to express it theatrically, my role was not even that of a spear carrier – scene shifter's assistant would be a more accurate description – but I believe I did make a contribution in training scores of officers and men to handle tank radio intelligently and I may have been of some use to senior staff officers at Eighth Army Headquarters where I was given the important sounding title of Captain Partridge, G.III Intelligence. I served for five years, four of them abroad in North Africa, Italy and Austria.

I had some unpleasant and dangerous moments, but could never bring myself to hate the German or Italian soldiers. I was shot at by an 88mm S.P. gun as I drove my scout car down a straight dusty track back from a forward position and I swear I was picked on by a Stuka bombing the road on my way back from seeing the North Irish Horse. I finished up with my scout car in the ditch several times but providentially, was never hit. I was one of many who 'never fired a shot in anger' which is one of the unthinking terms of derision reserved by front line troops for base wallahs. My anger was reserved for bullying NCOs and arrogant officers of whom there were one or two in most of our units.

On the whole, I enjoyed being involved with people of all ranks and meeting a very wide range of 'types' as Eighth Army officers in North Africa were called, and in situations which I would never have encountered at home in a hundred years. I gained a degree of confidence which helped when I began to move in the upper echelons of Fleet Street.

7

Master Printer. Jacob Kramer provides Art Education. On the Psychiatrist's Couch.

THE TRAIN which brought me back home from Villach to Calais, was pulled on different stretches of its journey by a variety of engines, including a wood-burning steam locomotive. I travelled some of the distance on the footplate with the driver who, at certain stages of the journey, nearly let the fire out so that the train lagged behind schedule. Then, he would stoke madly, burning forests of logs, and beam widely as the speedometer and clock showed him to be right back on schedule. The purpose of this technique, he informed me, was to ward off boredom on the long treks across Europe.

Eventually, I arrived at Aldershot where I was issued with a brown suit, coat, hat, shoes and a railway voucher to Richmond, Yorkshire. Betty met me at Darlington and after four years' separation, we started the long, slow process of getting to know each other again.

In 1946, I went back to my old job as a compositor at the *Daily Mail* where I was welcomed by Jack Jamieson with his usual good-natured disrespect: 'Here comes the fucking captain!'

I took lodgings in Withington. Betty and the children

stayed at 70 Frenchgate while I looked around for a better job where we could start our family life again. I had interviews at the *Northern Echo* in Darlington, the Oxford University Press, and several firms in Leeds: I was offered a post as a teacher of typography at the North Western Polytechnic of London but it was not to fall vacant until the following year and this was too late to be of any use to me.

I was promised the composing room overseer's job at the *Scottish Daily Mail* in Edinburgh. Betty travelled up in advance and rented a flat in Morningside which we had to cancel soon after because the Scottish printing trade union would not allow any more English union men into their select company. Finally, I left the *Mail* and went to Leeds to try and set up on my own. As a stop gap, I worked for a few months with E.J. Arnolds, the educational publishers and printers. We bought a house in Thorner in time to experience the very severe winter of 1947 when we skied for six weeks on the golf course and our old, wire-wheeled, high-off-the-ground Austin Seven, NJ 1518, was the only car to get up the hill out of the village for several days. Bob Stamp and I shared a composing frame at Arnolds. The work was simple and to avoid boredom, we sang Gilbert and Sullivan patter songs as we made up the pages of *Black Beauty* and *Young Lochinvar* in the *Bright Story Reader* series.

My brother Freddie had a garage in Leeds and with his help, I searched the district for a small printing business which we might buy. Eventually, I was introduced to George Hodgson who had a one-man printery which he wanted to sell so that he could retire. The price was £4,000. We raised this from our savings and war gratuity, took out a mortgage and a bank overdraft and bought the business, such as it was. The turnover was slightly less than the purchase price. Betty let some of our rooms to help pay the wages. The plant was a demy cylinder press, a foolscap folio platen, a hand-operated guillotine and a modest assortment of reasonable type, all housed on a rickety wooden first floor at 11 Craven Road in Woodhouse, Leeds.

One day, after about six months of struggling with new and unexpected problems I told Betty that there must be something seriously wrong with the set-up because I hadn't sung a note or whistled a tune since we took over from Hodgson, and this was very strange for me as I seemed to have been singing or whistling since I could remember. Then I began to suspect at least one reason why Hodgson had wanted to sell out. The foreman I had inherited proved to have an extraordinary talent for creating trouble for which he always appeared as the innocent party. On one occasion, he punched the apprentice, lifting him clean off his feet and across the room. He explained that the boy needed this treatment for his own good. Then he threatened to throw a customer down the stairs because he altered a proof twice.

I became very worried indeed but was reluctant to fire Charley whom I had known for years. Eventually I went to see our local doctor, Lawson, a sensible, six-foot-two, fourteen stone GP who had been an MO for the long Range Desert Group in North Africa. I told him about my work and that I was not sleeping at all well. He listened carefully, paused for a few moments and then wrote on his prescription pad, 'Sack your foreman.'

'Go now,' the wise doctor said. 'It's now 4.30, have him out by five o'clock, no messing about. Come back next week and I will tell you why. Here are six sleeping pills to help you over this weekend. That is all you are going to need.'

When I duly returned, Dr. Lawson said that the foreman was a case-book psychotic and a much more difficult problem than I could cope with. He had job after job during the next year; then he emigrated to Australia where I hoped his psychosis would be less noticeable.

My first years in business trading as Partridge Printers (Leeds) Ltd., were so difficult that on looking back I wonder why I ever stuck it. In the second year, I did actually go to see Frank Colebrook, the printers' auctioneer, to ask him to put up the business for sale. He was selling a printer's plant in Bradford. I stood at the back of the saleroom while he called for bids for Wharfedale and Heidelberg presses, waiting for the end of the sale before putting my proposition. Almost the final lot was an old linotype machine which was bought by a small printer in Harrogate whom I had known from school days. I asked myself that if he was buying machines, what was I doing trying to sell out? I walked away from the sale without speaking to anyone and went back to the works determined not to accept defeat.

The second year is the toughest one for a beginner in business. In the first year, you are not really aware of the problems; enthusiasm and innocence get you over the hurdles. In the second year, things beginners tend to ignore, like adequate working capital, come home with a vengeance until even the most benign of bank managers assumes the aspect of a hydra-headed monster.

When I started Partridge Printers, I was thirty-seven years old, a skilled craftsman with some staff experience in the Army. But there was so much more to learn here.

The scale of the business was small but the problems, as I saw them at the time, were enormous. More than once I stopped the car in a side street, biting back tears, almost defeated by complaining customers and people who wouldn't pay their bills. The greatest difficulty was caused by unpleasant clients for whom we were doing our best work but who, as a matter of apparent bargaining policy, criticised insignificant details until one's confidence was sapped. This is a problem particular to all small businesses where the boss is his own cost clerk, salesman and works manager. In a larger business, the problems are shared; the boss can be somewhat insulated from production problems and the salesman can refer at least some of the buyer's grumbles to the works manager.

I urgently set about filling gaps in my business education, reading the management pundits widely and attending residential courses at Grantley Hall, organised by Gavin Whittaker of Leeds University Economics faculty. These were not printers' courses, which I tended to shun, but were run for chemical engineers, mining managers and Coal Board officials.

Later on I returned to Grantley as an occasional lecturer on subjects relating to small businesses: sources of capital, cost of research and development and 'the problem of the burned-out supervisor'. I shared these sessions with Dr. Faulkner of ICI, Billingham, who employed 4,000 people. By now, I employed 40. We compared and contrasted our management styles. Dr. Faulkner was always clear of routine business by mid-morning and free to get around the plant or see visitors. His rule was that the deputies ran the business; he was there mainly to support and develop his successor, and to be the final court of appeal where his decision was crucial.

As the printing business developed, I was encouraged by comments in the trade press that a new printer in Leeds was doing good work. We received orders from the National Gallery, the Tate, and several fine art publishers in London which compensated for the appalling behaviour of some provincial advertising agents and publishers.

Once when I had been having trouble with Walter Neurath at the London publishers, Thames and Hudson, over colour matching, I took Tom Lambert, my very resourceful foreman, to see some of the original paintings in the National Gallery which we were reproducing. Neurath held my proofs to the window with the sun streaming down through the leaves of a plane tree and said, 'You're strong in the green, Partridge.' At the Gallery, Tom looked at his proofs and then at the original canvas and said, 'Titian didn't get a bad blue, did he?' The sequel to this intimate and friendly relationship with my foreman was very sad.

The firm grew in ten years from 40 employees to 150. It was taken over by Westminster Press and, in turn, took over three other printing businesses. Tom was a great craftsman and a fine small works manager. He established the high standard of printing on which the reputation of the firm was built, but he was eased out by Managing Director, Haydn Scott, on the grounds that his administrative abilities were inadequate. There is no compensation for loss of pride and Tom was greatly hurt. I am ashamed to say that I didn't do as much as I should have done to find him a suitable alternative post somewhere else in the group.

* * *

During its first ten years, the Leeds business grew steadily and became well known for good typography and fine printing. We had moved from Craven Road into the next street, Jubilee Terrace, where we bought a small factory and rented the defunct Electra Cinema next door, which had once been a Primitive Methodist Chapel. My office was in what had been the foyer; a small window in the wall had 'twopence' written over it, indicating the price of seats in the front stalls.

Over the office fireplace was an area of wall some three feet hight by eight feet long. One day, an elderly Leeds artist called Jacob Kramer, came in with me to see the works.

'What a marvellous space,' he said. 'I could do you something beautiful for a space like that. Something spiritual. I would do something Betty would like, really spiritual, if you just let me have thirty pounds to be going on with for materials.'

I provided the thirty pounds and the hardboard and size, not with any great optimism as to the outcome, but more to avoid causing Jacob the embarrassment of having to cadge thirty pounds to pay his rates. He knew this, and I knew it, but with oriental courtesy we gave and received this peck of patronage and remained good friends. Jacob always wanted to paint a picture for Betty and me that would be 'very spiritual'. He said this many times. At first I used to think that this was because he saw us as a religious family. We did attend church regularly at that time and I was involved in a certain amount of social 'good works' but we were never very devout. Then in 1960 when Herbert Read came to speak to the Yorkshire Luncheon Group, I learned exactly what Jacob meant by 'spiritual'. Read read to us extracts from a letter, 18 pages long, written to him by Jacob on March 10th, 1918:

'The degree of expression in a work of art,' Jacob wrote, 'is the measure of its greatness – a spiritual discernment is more essential than the reproduction of the obvious. If the expression is guided by deep emotion, I always find that I reproduce ... the reality. It is my endeavour to create a purely spiritual form, as it is only in this way that I can truthfully conform to my conception of expression.

'In my execution of a certain subject, I notice it is always natural for me to distinguish the spiritual from the actual, and also to separate them – both elements being derived from the same source, and the result is always conformity with realism itself. I always attain the utmost satisfaction in the portrayal of the purely spiritual. It signifies to me that the more conscious I become that the soul is being deeply moved, my very being vibrates with an intensity which produces a state of turmoil – I then direct myself towards a symbolical interpretation of the resultant emotion ... All my previous studies led me to perceive that only through symbolism could I express all the ideas that accumulated in the ordinary channels.'

And from a later page in the letter, this revealing sentence: 'The more conscious I become of the element of spirituality, which is inherent in everything, to that extent I am filled with a sense of abiding happiness which I am only capable of understanding when I express myself to the utmost.'

Just as Scriven introduced me to writers, particularly poets, it is to Kramer that I owe whatever acquaintance I may have with painters and paintings. He knew them all; had shared models with Jacob Epstein and a studio with Modigliani in Paris. Wyndham Lewis and the other Vorticists were his contemporaries (and friends, except perhaps Lewis, for whom he had little time). David Astor, Herbert Read and Flora Robson were also amongst his many friends.

Jacob Kramer was born at Klincy in the Ukraine in 1892. His father, Max Kramer, was a painter who had studied at St. Petersburg and his mother was a distinguished opera singer. Jacob told me that his father had to leave Russia because he was implicated in an anti-Czarist plot. This may have been a romanticised version of the facts. It is more likely that he left with thousands of other Jews in order to avoid conscription or the pogroms which periodically raged through Jewish settlements in the Ukraine.

Jacob's father set off in 1900 intending to go to New York. Due to an eye infection, he was refused an American visa and so went to Leeds where many Russian emigrés had settled to work and prosper in the clothing trade. Later on in the same year when Jacob was eight, he came with his mother to Leeds and, according to his own account, walked most of the way. His story of their exodus to the West always puts me in mind of Brecht's play *Mother Courage*, with the tough old woman dragging her household on a handcart across Europe.

At the age of fourteen, Jacob ran away from home and from Darley Street Council School and went to sea, sailing from Liverpool. After six months, he returned and got a job in Manchester, finally coming back to Leeds in 1907 when he won a senior scholarship to the Art School. In 1912, under the sponsorship of Michael Sadler and Sir William Rothenstein, he entered the Slade School in London, where some of his fellow students were David Bomberg, Mark Gertler, William Roberts, Stanley Spencer and Guevarah. Roberts married Jacob's sister, Sarah. The two brothers-in-law didn't get on well together.

When Jacob was seventy, I took him to see his sister in Little Venice, near Regent's Park. Jacob's by now almost monosyllabic trailing sentences made no breach in Roberts' paranoid suspicion and the two finished up glowering at each other from opposite corners of Sarah's basement kitchen, while she and I talked, and John, their son, who was a poet and professional guitarist, asked odd questions: 'Is he a lawyer?' – meaning me – 'What has he come for?'

While at the Slade, Jacob became very disturbed by the bullying of Bomberg and Roberts by Guevarah. Jacob was a big man with enormous hands and great strength. To put matters right at the Slade, he went to a boxing stable up the Mile End Road where he took lessons from Joe Beckett, the heavyweight champion. I asked Jacob why he went to this trouble on behalf of the weaker students. He said that they were all his friends, including Guevarah, but he wanted to teach him a sharp lesson without actually getting involved in an unseemly brawl. This he effected by knocking Guevarah unconscious with one cleanly-delivered right cross to the jaw. On another occasion, Jacob knocked out the tough South African poet, Roy Campbell, again in his role as champion of the oppressed.

Jacob got trapped in a particular style of impressionism and stood on the side lines of the London Group which made its mark on the art scene in 1910. He was finished as a painter when I first knew him in the 1950s. We grew to love and use each other as good friends do. I learned from him what little I know about painting and painters; he needed, in those failing years, the admiration and respect which I was able to give.

Although Jacob loved Leeds, a city which, to its eternal credit, took him to its heart and honoured him uncommonly well in his last few years, he liked to return to London occasionally for short visits. He had asked me many times to take him with me on one of my monthly selling trips. On one such visit, we arrived at the Waverley Hotel in Bloomsbury, a middling sort of place, handy for King's Cross and much frequented by visitors from the North. Jacob had his pyjamas in a minute fibre case, the sort of thing in which an apprentice might take his sandwiches to work in. He handed this to the hall porter, with Chaplinesque dignity, to carry in from the taxi, then we set off to see the Impressionists at the Tate Gallery.

As soon as we were there, Jacob settled himself down on a seat in front of a painting by Sisley. I walked round the gallery by myself for an hour, taking a quick look to see if I knew what I liked. When I returned to the first room, Jacob was still gazing at the Sisley. It was a small canvas showing some trees beside water. I asked if he wanted to see anything else.

'No,' he replied. 'I only want to see this one.'

'How do you rate the others?' I asked, indicating with a glance, the works of Monet, Cezanne, Manet and Degas.

'Pot boiler, pot boiler, good, pot boiler, fair, pot boiler,' he said, sticking out an accusing index finger from his enormous hand. 'But this one, this little Sisley, is a masterpiece. See how he has used his brushwork on the leaves, the delicacy, the way it picks up the light and lights up the picture.'

We then sought out the gallery director, Sir John Rothenstein, who had been helped by Jacob in his early days as director of the Leeds Art Gallery. Similarly at the National Gallery, later in the day, Jacob asked to see Mr. Hendy. The porter looked down his nose and said: 'Sir Phillip is out.'

Jacob put his foot in the door and replied: 'Then we'll wait.'

The parry and thrust of the request for an interview and refusal of entry went on for some time until, purely by chance, Sir Phillip's tall figure came striding down the passage towards us.

'Jacob, you old devil!' he shouted. 'What are you doing in London? Are you still hiding yourself away in Leeds? Why don't you come back? Why don't you come more often?'

Jacob shuffled his feet and smiled his shy smile and we went in for tea with Sir Phillip, another great director who had been glad of Jacob's counsel when he was a young man in Leeds.

That evening, Jacob and I walked for miles along the square streets of Soho: Greek Street, Frith Street, Romilly Street, Old Compton Street. We ate at Blooms and drank at the Fitzroy.

'This is where old so-and-so shot himself. This is where the model I shared with Sickert was found stabbed. I saw the blood coming under the door. I stepped over her body, collected my things and left. I never went back.'

Jacob relived episodes from the 1910 period and gave me a running commentary as we slowly trod the wet, black pavements.

In later life, as his talent diminished, Jacob was short of friends and in a sincere and mutual friendship, I seemed able to fill a gap. In art education and perception, being taught not only to look but to see, I benefitted immeasurably.

We never got our spiritual mural for the printing office in Jubilee Terrace. Two years after it was commissioned I peeped at the eight foot by three foot hardboard as it leaned face to the wall in Jacob's studio at the bottom of Mount Preston behind Leeds Town Hall. The blank board carried one short black crayon mark, boomerang-shaped, about nine inches long. When Jacob died, the work had progressed no further.

* * *

In 1964 I had my first, and up to now, only contact with the psychiatrist's couch. The treatment was brief, spectacular and successful. It happened during the time I was managing the printing contract of *The Observer* as well as holding the chairmanship of Beck and Partridge, now a fast-growing company in Leeds, and while I was being courted by the *Financial Times* to manage their printing activities at St. Clements Press. The problem was not one of overwork but was due to the fact that I was not quite tough enough to cope with some of the infighting which is endemic to Fleet Street management.

I don't think anyone except Betty had any idea what a state I used to get into, until I occasionally blew my top and tore into some unsuspecting colleague, usually a senior director. If I could have done this to order, it might have been quite effective therapy; in fact, it did often clear the air and rid me of frustration, but sometimes this temperamental behaviour was just foolish and certainly counter-productive.

One of our new friends in London was Robert Ollendorf, a doctor who lived in Camberwell Grove. Robert was a psychiatrist, general practitioner and dyed-in-the-wool anarchist. As a medical student in Germany in the thirties, he had been actively anti-Nazi, and being a Jew, eventually had to get out to survive. First, he visited Italy to stay with family friends; then, when this proved to be less than useful as Italy became more and more fascist, he travelled to Central Africa where he worked for a construction company as a medical officer.

After the war, Ollendorf qualified at Leeds University Medical School, and moved on to Cambridge for further studies. At a later stage, he studied psychiatry in Sweden (I think this was under his brother-in-law, Wilhelm Reich) and became an advocate of vegetotherapy, which, as I understood it, set out to establish the sensible rule that mind and body cannot entirely be separated in any form of medical or psychiatric treatment. At that time, they were treated separately or, rather, psychiatry was largely ignored throughout medical training in Britain. Ollendorf was engaged in a running battle with the British Medical Association on this issue.

One evening, while at dinner with the Ollendorfs, Robert was holding forth on the damage done to mental health by prudes and puritans in general, and 'bloody Methodists' in particular. This latter criticism hit me on a tender spot. My parents were devout chapel folk who had struggled through a hard life to give a large family a decent upbringing. I listened to Robert's blaspheming for a while, then my safety catch of politeness slipped and I fired off a furious salvo attacking his ignorance of chapel-based, Northern working-class culture, of which he had no experience and no understanding. My unseemly outburst stopped the conversation until Robert's sister, Mrs. Reich and his wife, Kirstie, guided us back to civility. After the meal, Robert took me by the arm and led me into his surgery.

'Get your clothes off and get on that couch!' he ordered.

While the others were enjoying Kirstie's delicious coffee, Robert was pulling out the joints of my fingers and toes, pressing on my ribs and twisting my neck round like someone trying to tear a stick from a hazel bush.

'Stop it!' I shouted. 'You're hurting me.'

'I know. I meant to,' Robert said. 'Why are you clenching your toes like this?'

'I'm not clenching them,' I told him. 'Can't you see, I've got ten hammer toes. Born with them. They run in the family. I had six fingers as well and my children have twelve toes.'

'Rubbish! Your neck is stiff with calcium and your ribs are rigid like metal rods instead of flexible like bamboo as they should be. Who are you defending yourself against? Who are these bloody directors you keep talking about, Lord bloody this and Duke bloody that?!'

The kneading, pulling and twisting continued in spite of my shouts.

'You take care of Betty and your family,' Robert said, 'and to hell with their lordships in Fleet Street!'

I went back to him a week later for another session of

agony on the couch which by now, I had learned to recognise as vegetotherapy, a form of physio-psychotherapy. And that was enough. The cure was complete. A miracle cure, if ever there was one, for my high tension and tantrums. Or maybe I became too frightened of the treatment to let the symptoms show any more. Either way, I got life and work back into a decent balance and perspective, apart from the occasional lapse: like the time I drove my car from outside Ollendorf's house slap across Camberwell Grove, over the pavement, through a privet hedge and on to the lawn of the house opposite. The lady on whose lawn I had landed threw up her window and cried out in horror.

'Sorry, madam,' I said to her. 'I am just visiting the gentleman opposite.'

I reversed into the road and drove off. Later I telephoned the lady to apologise and sent her a cheque to pay for the damaged hedge.

In spite of these incidents, the Ollendorfs became close friends. One day when I had dropped in for a drink after work, Robert asked me to try out the Orgone Box. This was a black wooden construction the size of a telephone kiosk and designed like a one-man privy, with a peephole the size of a small letter box cut in the door (reminding me of a three-man privy I once sat in at a farm in Langdale in the twenties!). The Orgone Box was a device conceived by Wilhelm Reich in America. He claimed that it would concentrate psychic energy out of the ether. I can't recall the mystical psycho-jargon used by Reich and his followers to describe the cause and effect of the Box's life-enhancing powers. It is all fully explained in a biography of Reich by Colin Wilson, *In Search of Wilhelm Reich.*

Reich promoted and sold the Box for the treatment of various conditions, including cancer and certain neuroses; this lead to an investigation by the U.S. Food and Drug Administration in 1947, and to his eventual prosecution and imprisonment. Reich warned his persecutors and prosecutors that General Eisenhower's bombers were secretly protecting him and watching over him all the time! He died in an American federal penitentiary in 1957, still the victim of delusions.

I don't know where he got it but Robert had one of these now legendary Boxes in his surgery. I was told to get inside it and sit quietly for five minutes. It was supposed to raise my temperature a degree or two, increase my pulse rate and illuminate my perceptions – a bit like LSD. None of these things happened. Actually, I felt chilly and my pulse and temperature remained as they were. I didn't see visions or dream dreams – in fact, being always a touch claustrophobic, I was glad to get out.

Not for the first time, Robert was disappointed in me. I told him that I thought the Orgone Box was a load of old rubbish and that five quiet minutes in a Quaker or Methodist prayer meeting would do his patients more good! But I was totally converted to his vegetotherapy theory, physical manipulation to ease up the calcified joints and his stern talk about the folly of false gods: money, fame, success, pride, and trying to please all of the people all of the time.

I regarded the Orgone Box as pure witchcraft. Ollendorf would have said the same about the Eucharist which I now attend in Salisbury Cathedral on Sunday mornings. There is certainly magic in the bread and wine, but unlike Reich's absolution, it works for me. The brief vegetotherapy treatment also worked. Instead of being an impatient semi-neurotic, I began to achieve a decent balance in life after only two short sessions on Ollendorf's couch. The message seemed to be, 'You can't treat the body without looking into the mind, and you certainly can't treat the mind without consideration of the body.'

Wilhelm Reich's concern was with the damage done to human personality and behaviour by 'biological expression' – the defensive armour and rigidity, the physical posture which people adopt as protection for their social vulnerability. He used the term 'the armoured individual' to describe the attitude of 'holding back' – 'shoulders pulled back, the thorax pulled up, the chin held rigid, respiration shallow, lower back arched ...'

Reich is describing the defensive stance which so many of us adopt at times of stress and which do nothing to ease the situation but, in fact, make matters worse and can cause serious psychological harm.

I'll go along with that.

8

Travels in America.
'Don't Hang Your Hat Too High'

THERE WERE many times in the years between 1963 and 1969 when I felt that I had entered myself in the wrong race: the jumps were too high and the course too long. Technical matters I found easy to resolve, financial questions could usually be answered with a fairly positive yes or no, but the bitchiness of some people at all levels in business often caused me to question seriously whether the game was worth the candle.

Fortunately, the bad times were compensated for by good friendships made both at home and on my various trips abroad, taken in a continuous search for improved methods of producing newspapers.

In September 1964, I travelled to New York to attend the first of a series of seminars organised by a young prophet of advanced technology, John Diebold.

The U.S. space programme and military information systems were highly developed by this time and part of the justification for their enormous budgets – the military had just spent five hundred million dollars on hardware and forty million dollars on programming alone – was the spin-off to industry.

John Diebold had persuaded a dozen of the world's largest newspaper proprietors, and an equal number of press makers and computer suppliers, to meet in order to discuss what the publishers thought they wanted from new technology and what the engineers and computer people felt they might be able to provide. These were early days in the application of data processing, particularly to a traditional craft-based industry like printing which had changed little between 1900 and 1950. Our discussions were centred on 'total information systems' — the organisation of editorial input, setting, printing and distribution of newspapers based on computer technology. We had a new jargon to learn which greatly amused Dr Tom Margerison, one of the London contingent, but within two years, the new vocabulary was totally absorbed into our everyday speech.

We were concerned with information for management as well as editing and production. Under the guidance of the Diebold team, we designed a block diagram of the ideal 'total system' with its large central processor. Input would be from on-line news services, on-line copy takers, OCR (optical character recognition) devices for reporters' copy. Classified advertisements would be costed out and credit checked before being transferred from a display unit to the central data store. Output would be full-page make-up via cathode ray tube character generators and digital display units. Laser type setting soon followed.

All this sounded a bit far fetched in 1964 when we sat around discussing it, with Tom Margerison teasing the very serious American computer priesthood like a rather wicked schoolmaster. Now, in the 1980's, the whole business is commonplace in newspaper houses. Front runners in this technical revolution were *The Wall Street Journal*, John Perry Publications, Palm Beach, and *The*

Miami Herald. I visited these and many other firms before setting up the first data processing team at the *Financial Times* under Lee Tate, now managing director of a large international computer company.

On my first trip to New York in September, 1964, we flew over Newfoundland which looked waterlogged and desolate; turned half-left over Boston, with Cape Cod seventy miles away on the port side, and landed at Kennedy Airport after seven hours' flying time in a Boeing 707. I was met by one of Bowaters' New York men, in a Cadillac long enough to please a Persian Princess, and taken to the Drake Hotel. After a meal, I walked to a bar outside Grand Central Station where I tried, and failed, to buy a scotch and soda without ice. (I wasted a lot of time on that visit trying to buy drinks without ice).

'Just arrived?' enquired the barman.

'Yes,' I replied.

'From London?'

'Yes.'

'Well, mister' he said, in a low confidential voice, looking up and down the long bar. 'You shouldn't walk around alone at night, and you shouldn't take more cash with you than you need for the evening.'

'I haven't much money, really,' I said.

'You've got two hundred and twenty-five dollars,' he told me, with alarming accuracy. 'And don't walk home from here, take a cab. I'll call you one. I'm not the only one in this bar who's sized you up and counted your cash.'

Next day, to recover from jet lag, I took a walk round the streets off Park Avenue. The buildings were fantastic – like towering cliffs on either side. I was reminded of my feelings when I first saw Venice in 1945: I had expected it to be beautiful but was staggered by its actual beauty. In New York I had a similar sensation for a different reason: I had expected tall buildings, but the vertical scale of the city's architecture took my breath away. New York has style rather than beauty. Dust and noise and wind blight the place. The Pan Am building, a mind-and-vision-blocking concrete cliff face, should never have been allowed; it turns Park Avenue into an optical cul-de-sac. I ate an indifferent meal at the Waldorf Astoria, then took a taxi to tour the city. My driver was true to the garrulous reputation of his kind. I learned that his father came from Palermo and that he was brought up in the Italian quarter of New York; he described how all the national quarters in the city were separate and the inhabitants bilingual. He confirmed that it was unsafe to walk near Central Park at night, or, in fact, to walk alone in any quiet street after dark.

'I could get you moidered any time for five dollars or ten reefers,' he told me. 'Easy, any time.'

All of which was calculated to make the ride more interesting.

We saw Wall Street and Orchard Street in the Jewish quarter with its stalls on the pavement – very special. In Chinatown, we caught glimpses of an election campaign but otherwise this seemed to be the most peaceful, law-abiding part of the city. Harlem was a tough quarter, as was the Puerto Rican area on the west side of Central Park, around 100 to 110th Street. At the docks on the Hudson River, ocean liners like the QUEEN ELIZABETH and the UNITED STATES were dwarfed by the towering backcloth of piled-up buildings, making them look the size of Thames River launches. A drought had made Central Park a dry scab on the city floor. My driver lived twenty miles out and told me that he had two peach trees and two pear trees in a 50 × 100 yards garden. Although New York City bred, he wouldn't live there now.

'The trouble with New York,' he said, when I had complained about the permanent roar of traffic and the air conditioning plant that woke me every day at 4 a.m., 'the trouble with New York is there's no peace no place. The police are sloppy, low grade characters. They all take graft, to a man. That's the only reason for joining; a lazy job with plenty of graft perks.'

The next time I went to New York for a Diebold seminar, I awoke on the first day with a temperature of 102°. The hotel captain called a doctor who prescribed two aspirins four times a day and charged forty dollars for the visit. I stayed in bed for two days until I was down below 100°. The Diebold people sent me flowers, which I thought a rather melancholy gesture. I ate melon and drank champagne and on the third day, flew home again.

In 1965, my American trip was more successful. This time I visited *The Wall Street Journal* offices in New York and South Brunswick. I went to Washington D.C., Louisville in Kentucky, Miami and Palm Beach, in search of higher technology, and scotch without ice.

In Louisville, I saw Stravinsky conduct *The Rite of Spring* and *The Firebird* in a vast auditorium which looked and sounded like a drill hall built for championship boxing. The old maestro leaned on the rostrum: I prayed that it would be strong enough to hold up his frail figure until the final bar.

The following evening, I was taken by Lisle Baker, a

director of the *Louisville Courier Journal*, to an election meeting – complete with bands, balloons and dancing girls – and introduced as a representative of the British press to Senator Robert Kennedy, brother of the assassinated President, John F. Kennedy. Bobby Kennedy was there in support of another Democratic Senate candidate.

'What did you think of the show?' the handsome, toothy young hero asked me. 'Do you have anything like this in English elections?'

'No,' I replied, without batting an eyelid, 'We have a lot to learn.'

The 'show' had opened with prayers and continued for two hours with a mixture of something like the last night at the Proms, a children's pantomime and a revivalist rally.

A few years later, Bobby Kennedy was the second assassination victim in this tragic family.

After several meetings at the *Courier Journal* and a trip through the Blue Grass country to a prohibition township where we swigged Bourbon out of ice cream cartons in the lavatory, I flew on to Miami to see what was then the most technically advanced publishing operation in the world. The *Miami Herald* is housed in a superb building with an art gallery in the entrance hall and one-inch thick pale blue armour-plated glass walls facing the beach.

'Why armour-plated?' I asked. 'Is this in case Castro comes?'

'No,' was the reply. 'When the hurricanes come, it's protection against their blowing coconuts off the trees and stones off the beach.'

There can be no doubt that I was the whitest man in

the hotel swimming pool. I bought myself a pair of Bermuda shorts and sat on a stool at the bar, drinking a very long gin and tonic. The man sitting on the stool next to me, sipping his Tom Collins, was a tall, bronzed type, looking like an ageing John Wayne.

'On holiday?' he asked, after we had sat in discreet silence for two drinks.

'Part holiday, part business,' I answered.

'What business?'

'Printing newspapers.'

'I own three newspapers,' he volunteered, adding in a sort of nonchalant, insignificant way, 'and a bank.'

Not to be totally outdone, I informed him that I had, until recently, owned a printing works, but had sold out to a group which I had then joined in the role of technical development manager; a job, I added, that seemed to suit my temperament better. I had run out of growth capital and not managed to borrow enough from the banks to build up Partridge Printers fast enough.

'You made three mistakes,' he said, now taking on the mantle of a psychiatrist treating a harmless patient. 'First: never borrow from a bank. They can get you by the balls. Always borrow on the golf course. There your friends can't let you down. You spread the risk and they can't get out. Second: you didn't go bankrupt soon enough.'

'I didn't go bankrupt,' I protested.

'No, but you should have done. In the second year. Then you learn the hard lessons early on and come back saying to hell with everyone but me. You gotta come back fighting or you won't survive.'

We had another round on the strength of the treatment so far. Then I asked, without looking at my counsellor:

'What's the third mistake I made?'

'You ain't predatory,' he said, quietly, putting both feet on the ground and strolling off – leaving me to pick up the bill.

After a lot of difficulty with the Hertz people who didn't want cash – and I hadn't got the right credit card – I hired a car and drove to Palm Beach.

'How the hell do we know who you are without a Diners or American Express card?' protested the Hertz man as I presented British passport, business card, letter of introduction from the *Financial Times*, and a wad of dollar bills. I had three hours in Palm Beach: one of them at Perry Publications and two, sheltering from a tropical storm, eating a chicken salad in a French restaurant. I never saw the beach.

John Perry was a pioneer in the automation of newspaper production. He also designed and built one-man submarines. His dedication to computer-assisted typesetting was the result of a running battle he had had with the Typographers Union. They had closed him down at one of his numerous regional printing centres, so he set out not just to reduce his staff of compositors but to eliminate them altogether. When I went into what had been the composing room, a machine was sucking in sheets of editorial copy, passing it through an electronic reader and a computer film setter, and turning out columns of typematter on film at the far end. Between the copy input and the columns of typeset matter coming out, there was just one girl, drinking coffee.

Outside the front door, a man stood with placards fore and aft bearing the message: 'This shop is black.'

'Why is it black?' I asked.

'Because it doesn't use Typographers Union compositors.'

'How long has it been blacked?'

'Two and a half years.'

'Why are you doing this, standing here in the rain?'

'I get more pay from the union doing this than my brother does and he's a printing foreman.'

When I sat down with John Perry in his office, I asked him what was the position in his industrial dispute with the Typographers Union.

'Not too bad,' he said.

'But you've got a picket on the front door.'

'Is he still there? Well, it's like this. We've reached a satisfactory compromise. He gets on with his picketing and we get on with our newspaper printing with no interference. The picket man comes into the canteen for his lunch every day.'

Somebody, I thought, deserves a Nobel Prize for this piece of industrial diplomacy.

One day I was waiting for the rain to stop outside a restaurant in Palm Beach and fell into conversation with a very black looking Mr.Smith of Nassau, who was down there having a few weeks' holiday.

'I was born a bastard,' he said with some pride. 'Of a wicked mother. I ran away from home in New York at the age of ten and I now own five houses in Brooklyn. I deals in property and runs a car hire fleet of nine limousines for weddings and funerals.'

'You've done well,' I said.

'Yes, I've done pretty well. I'm sixty-nine. I can eat and drink anything, and screw six times a week. I read the Bible every day and pray God for peace of mind. My lesson is, young fellow, never hang your hat too high. Sisal grows only three feet tall but if you weave it end on end, you can make it reach the whole length of the street.'

He smiled a wide smile, showing a large expanse of pale pink gum above and below his piano key teeth. He reached out his pale palm for a big pump handle handshake.

'Never hang your hat too high, my friend,' he repeated and shuffled off as the hot sun broke through.

* * *

In July 1967, I decided to leave the *Financial Times.* The commercial printing division had been closed down; the computer team I had recruited, led by Lee Tate, had been frustrated for two years in its efforts to modernise FT production and to set up, jointly with other institutions, a computerised market information service which would have included audio and visual response to on-line interrogation. The FT prices pages were still being set by hand in typefounder's type, letter by letter, every day. The dinosaur-like attitudes of Fleet Street printing unions prevented any move into the now well-established techniques of electronic editing and computer typesetting. I met with the Group Chairman, Lord Gibson, and got myself transferred from the FT to its sister company, Westminster Press (Provincial Newspapers) Limited.

There was an earlier Westminster Press, distinguished for design and typography if not for commercial success, housed at 411a Harrow Road and owned successively by Wilfred and Gerard Meynell, of whose family Wyndham Lewis is quoted as having said: 'Blast Clan Meynell!'

The Westminster Press with which I was concerned had no connection with 'Clan Meynell' and even less with fine typography. It was, like the *Financial Times*, Lazard's Bank and many other publishing and industrial companies, part of Lord Cowdray's family business — the Pearson Group.

The first Viscount Cowdray (Weetman Pearson) was a nineteenth century entrepreneur in the classic mode who had built up an international civil engineering business — S. Pearson & Son Ltd. — with achievements that included the construction of the Blackwall Tunnel, the Mexican Grand Canal and the Sennar Dam across the Blue Nile. Pearson was one of a group of prominent Liberals who had owned the *Westminster Gazette* since 1908. By the end of the 1914–18 war, he had become, for practical purposes, its sole proprietor. Westminster Press Limited was formed in 1920 with Weetman Pearson as its chairman. The new company soon acquired newspaper businesses in many parts of the country including companies previously owned or controlled by the Rowntree Trust, Sir Charles Starmer and others. The remarkable drive and business acumen of Weetman Pearson is recorded in a biographical study by Desmond Young published under the title, *Member for Mexico* (Cassells, 1966). There can be little doubt that some of his commercial talent has been handed down to the third generation of the family.

Westminster Press is now associated, through Pearson Longman, with large-scale book publishing and it directly controls more than a hundred regional newspapers up and down the country, including the *Northern Echo*, the *Bradford Telegraph* and the *Oxford Mail*. During the merger of this extended newspaper group, the company had acquired, not always enthusiastically, a number of general printing businesses which had been, at an earlier time, the dogs on which a newspaper was the tail. Now the tail wagged the dog. The decline of these jobbing print firms, loosely held together in what was called the Printing Group, was the result of a long run down, with the proprietors applying the generally wise business maxim of putting their capital investment and best available management skills where the best profits were likely to be made. This was in newspapers, not general printing.

I was appointed chairman of the Printing Group which now included Partridge Printers in Leeds. My intended policy for the Printing Group was to develop three main printing centres in Edinburgh, Leeds and Uxbridge, each specializing in one particular branch of the trade: books, fine art printing and publicity, and to siphon the less successful divisions into these three, or close them down.

We bought the fine, old, established, Edinburgh book printing business, T & A Constable, and merged into it the production departments of Oliver & Boyd and the Darian Press. The publishing functions of these businesses were taken into Longmans. In Leeds, we bought the 200-year-old colour printing firm of Beck & Inchbold, mainly for its excellent site and modern building. Partridge Printers, Byles of Bradford and Beck & Inchbold were amalgamated into a new company housed at the Beck location in Seacroft under Haydn Scott, as managing director, who had managed the Partridge business since 1960. The merger was accompanied by high-minded statements in the trade press about a more secure future for all in the larger enterprise, but, in the end, things didn't work out as well as I had hoped.

The quality of the work done was excellent, in letterpress, offset and screen printing; the design studio produced excellent work and was a great credit to the firm. In the early 70s, a great deal of time, effort and capital went into the development of heat transfer printing for the garment industry, a bold move showing once again Scott's enterprise. Profits, on the other hand, were always patchy and, throughout the 60s, failed to average a figure equal to the bank rate, which is a poor way to use shareholders' capital. In the combined businesses, both management and shop floor staffs came in for a rough ride. Ex-proprietors and managers of the previous companies were paid up and removed, one by one, as Scott found them unacceptable.

For several years Westminster Press had been trying to sell the general printing businesses, at almost any price, in order to concentrate their resources on the more profitable newspaper companies. This was not good for morale in my general printing division and I was not surprised when Scott said that he was planning to start out on his own in heat transfer printing. What came as a surprise was the way he did it: taking with him six of the company's senior staff and most of the turnover, leaving the company stripped of its senior management and main customers.

Meanwhile, at Westminster Press, we had merged three plants in Edinburgh, sold off the Swindon and Bath printing businesses and shut down Dressers of Darlington. In trying to manage this situation, I found myself to be as miscast as anyone possibly could be. I had a series of shouting matches with the Group chairman, and resigned three times in one week! He said I was a collapsed manager and a failed executive and that I had better shut up and get on with managing properly, or get out. Having established who was on top in the pecking order, we exchanged little notes of apology and regret: I, for my unseemly behaviour, he for perhaps not having conveyed in our interviews the regard in which he held me. My face was saved and my esteem for RPT Gibson went back up again.

The final outcome resulted in the Duke of Atholl succeeding me as chairman of the Printing Group: I remained as his assistant and printing consultant to the Group with permission to do freelance work on my own account. This arrangement worked well. I had lowered my sights and was now shooting at targets within my own range.

Ian Atholl, the most reasonable and kindly of colleagues, told me that he valued being in the House of Lords because it had the most convenient car park in central London. He invited Betty and me to stay overnight at Blair Castle when he and I were attending a board meeting at Constables in Edinburgh. We were collected from Waverley Station and taken to the castle where the Duke commands his own private army of Highlanders. We dined in modest splendour (the paradox is intended) and retired to our room with its fourposter bed and a bath which was climbed into by a small flight of four steps. When the enormous taps were turned on, an absolute Niagara Falls of near-boiling water gushed out.

We admired the long row of stags' heads lining the upstairs corridor and the housekeeper told us a sad tale of good intentions gone wrong. One day when the family were away, she decided to wash the antlers. They had been collecting grime and dust for a long time. She filled one of the great baths with warm water and plenty of detergent, took down six of the heads and placed them in the bath. Returning after an hour or more to rinse and replace them with the next six monarchs of the glen, she was devastated to find a jumbled heap of eyes, teeth and antlers at the bottom of the bath. The glue had melted.

The path of technical evolution is strewn with the corpses of traditional craftsmen and conservative managements. It probably took a thousand years for a flint arrowhead to acquire its barb, and five hundred years for a cylinder printing machine to be developed from the common flat platen press. Hand-set single characters of type made up the pages of books and newspapers from Gutenberg's Mainz press in 1450 to the end of the 19th century. From 1900 we are into another story, first of technical change, then of revolution. Mechanisation was in full swing. Monotype and Linotype were in common use; offset was challenging letterpress. But many small printers continued to make a living with plant that would not have seemed strange to Caxton.

For fifty years into the new century changes took place gradually. Then an electronic blizzard swept through printing and publishing, wiping out five centuries of accumulated skills like cobwebs before a vacuum cleaner.

Now, in the 'nineties, lead type is for the museum and letterpress for therapy. Pages of text and pictures are generated in seconds by computer-driven laser beams. We now have non-impact ink-jet printing, and soon the impressionless non-stop data-stream press, able at the touch of a key, to switch pages or change editions without stopping the press.

This is the end of the Gutenberg era.

9

Retirement to Wiltshire. Starting a Private Press.

Napoleon may have been right if he had said that the English were a nation of shopkeepers: the remark is attributed to him but was actually written by Adam Smith when Napoleon was five years old. What is certain is that if the English succeed in shopkeeping, or any other trade, they soon want to be country gentlemen. Snobbery, not perfidy, is the English vice.

I never bought a horse or rode to hounds like Jorrocks but I did conform enough to the pattern by moving out of London to Wiltshire. I bought a farmhouse and a few acres where I could have space to develop some retirement hobbies and take the dog for a walk in the woods without driving miles in a car. I started a private press, filled a big barn with Victorian printing presses, collected books, planted trees and fished the river Nadder for trout.

I decided to semi-retire at 60, by leaving printing management and going into consultancy. I was already retained by a few firms to give commercial and technical advice and this necessitated my living within two hours' travelling distance of London so that I could get in for mid-morning meetings.

I drew circles on a map marking half-hour distances

from Charing Cross, going out to a 120 mile perimeter. We looked at Essex and East Anglia and were not impressed; we had days out and pub lunches in the Surrey belt, taking in the Dorking and Guildford areas, and found the communities neatly separated into the bridge and golf set, and the peasantry. Pub bars were actually separated to foster this social division which we found unacceptable. We looked at Lulworth and the Blackmore Vale in Dorset. This was more to our liking, and met many of our needs, but it was half an hour too far out.

When we saw an advertisement in *Trout and Salmon* for a mill house at Tisbury in the Nadder Valley, Wiltshire, this looked about right. The countryside was hilly and streamy like the parts of Yorkshire and Sussex where we were brought up. The train from Tisbury to Waterloo took one and a half hours. The pubs were friendly, and there was much to occupy the ageing ex-executive. The mill had buildings which would make a printing shop; there was the river and small ponds for a trout hatchery.

We agreed a price, having decided to buy, but our solicitor warned us against going ahead. Apparently the deeds were fraught with legal complexities over riparian rights, and he could foresee writs flying to and fro at regular intervals. A previous owner, an engineer, had re-opened an ancient mill but without planning consent, in order to drive a turbine to generate electricity for the house. This fresh mill-race was threatening to disturb the water table in the up-stream meadows to the annoyance of the farmer, who was considering legal action. So we bowed out of the deal and looked lower down the valley.

At Chicksgrove, two miles from Tisbury, we talked to a farmer who said that his downstream neighbour had a derelict mill that he might be persuaded to part with. Spencer's Mill at Sutton Mandeville is recorded in the Domesday Book as having a meadow and a wood worth ten shillings. It has a lovely position on the Nadder and although it was no longer used to grind flour – that had ceased in the 1940s – the water wheel did turn and hornbeam spurs on the gear wheel quietly engaged with iron bevel gears to drive a barley crusher which produced cattle feed.

The mill was not for sale. The cottage roof had fallen in and nobody lived there but it was not for sale. However, the owner told us that his uncle, who lived up the hill next to the church, often complained of his health and said he was thinking of selling up and moving to the coast.

'Don't go just now,' the mill owner cautioned. 'I'll give you a ring next time he talks about selling. I could do with a few more acres. Maybe we could share the land if you were able to buy the farm.'

Which is what we did. Church Farm – formerly part of the Wyndham Estate – comprised a four-bedroom farmhouse with adjoining cottage, probably rebuilt around 1800 on a much earlier foundation, in local Chilmark stone, and to use estate agents language, spacious and commodious outbuildings, an attractively laid out garden and 36 acres of land including 300 yards of river frontage to the Nadder. I went to see Mr. Green, the owner, and told him I was looking for somewhere to live in that area. He said he was thinking of moving. Would we like to come in and look at the house?

The asking price was £28,000 for the lot. Robert

Jeffrey, the selling agent, didn't have to ask twice. We sold off 27,282 acres to the Spencers in 1971 for £9,350 and bought six acres of woodland from Maurice Hankey, a neighbour up the hill, for £1,250 in July of the same year.

For the next few years, with the help of Hedley Weeks, a craftsman builder from Downton, we worked on the property during holidays and weekends while still living in our flat at Eyott Lodge in Twickenham. The small rooms were opened up to make fewer but larger spaces; a studio was built in place of an old ground floor bedroom; the cottage was given a pitched roof to replace its previous flat concrete slab. Mr. Weeks put in a new kitchen which he designed on the lime-washed walls with a stub of joiner's pencil:

'Cupboards here, about this size, worktop along here, cupboards under opening this way; uncover and re-glaze this bricked-up window,' and so on.

We didn't ask for a quotation of cost but gave Mr. Weeks a budget of £2000 and said 'when you look like coming to the end of that amount, ask for another sum.' A vast amount of restoration work was done, including re-roofing and putting new floors into the big barn. The total cost came out at something like £7000.

We finished up with a farmhouse and cottage listed as being of architectural and historical interest, with 15 acres of grazing and woodland, for an overall cost of under £30,000. The house had been thatched: an early photograph of the property shows it looking like a scene from a Hardy novel or a William Barnes poem. Now it is tiled. There was a lawn at the side, an orchard at the front and we carved a kitchen garden out of the field at the back, which had at one time been a large cider apple orchard. We bought an old cider press and, for a few years, made our own scrumpy. The farm yard and buildings were on the north side between the house and All Saints Church, Sutton Mandeville, which is on the site of an earlier Saxon church. Traces of the round Saxon graveyard were found beyond the walled boundary of the Norman church, of which the tower still stood. The nave had been repaired and mostly rebuilt by a builder, Mr. Miles, of Shaftesbury in 1862. The first rector was Albertus in 1130, a century before the building of the Cathedral at New Sarum, now called Salisbury.

One day, a local builder and his apprentice came to rebuild a fallen section of the churchyard wall. As they dug down for a new foundation, the boy struck what he took to be a root from the big yew tree nearby. He heaved it out and found an ankle joint at one end and a knee at the other. His ruddy complexion cooled to a pale grey for a little while. We christened the deceased Herbert, put all the bits of him that we could find into a wooden box, and re-interred him on the right side of the wall.

There was a well, fifty feet deep, by our front gate. This was worked with an electric pump and supplied water to the house, so analytically pure that it could have been bottled and sold as spa water. Across the lawn there was the old village Pound where stray cattle used to be impounded until they were claimed by their owners and a small 'poundage' paid to the constable. We planted a rhododendron hedge, a few apple trees and a young tulip tree in the pound to mark the year of Queen Elizabeth II's Silver Jubilee.

Sutton Mandeville, now more a scattered hamlet than a village, used to have a school, two shops, a working flour mill and a Silver Prize band in which Alby Spencer played the cornet when he was a boy. He was about eighty when I used to call on him in his cottage with its decayed thatch at the top of Mill Lane. He showed me relics from his childhood which I imagine would have been lost by the time the cottage collapsed two or three years after his death.

Mrs. Winifred Johnson lived at 'The Homestead' until she handed it over to her son, Terry, and moved into their nearby cottage next door to Mrs. Lodge. Both ladies were about 1900 vintage; vigorous, articulate, sometimes quarrelsome and as tough as old boots. They argued with each other over the fence as to which of them would last the longest.

'I'll see you into your grave,' challenged Mrs. Lodge.

'I'll see you in hell first!' replied Mrs. Johnson.

Mrs. Johnson was the survivor.

Every autumn, Jim Spencer, a local farmer, came to ask if they could 'walk through' our few acres of woodland and pasture. The 'walk through' was a farmer's shoot, when the Spencers and half a dozen friends would hold a shoot through the surrounding woods and fields. A 'shoot' is perhaps a bit of an understatement for what looked and sounded like a platoon of partisans blasting away at anything that moved. I wouldn't have given much for the chances of even a sitting pheasant when the Sutton shoot was on the attack.

The wood on Harris's Hill, a plateau behind the house, was a mixture of trees, mostly conifers, planted during the Second World War when the oaks were felled for some military purpose; not, I think, for building ships, but you never know with our Ministry of Defence. There were a few old oaks and wild cherries of enormous height and girth, certainly 80 feet high and six feet around the butt. We planted another hundred mixed oaks and beeches at the top of the hill which had been left to brambles and willows when the big trees were taken out. Although there were only about eight acres of trees, I cleared a pattern of footpaths around and across so that it was possible to have a nature walk without covering the same path twice, marking some of the paths with Norwegian maples. Roe deer wandered through and a badger famly, with its tidy latrine area, had a sett and a long traceable route to other parts of the village.

Out of an escarpment on the north side of the hill there flowed a pure spring which remained at a constant, cool temperature, winter and summer, and fed a stream flowing down into the Nadder. Mrs. Johnson told me that when she was a child, people used to come with bottles and take the water away for eye lotion.

During the '70s, my son, Nicolas, found a polished flint axe sticking up through the pine needles near a track in the wood close to the corner of Collinsplatt's big field. Another granular stone axe was discovered two feet down when we were digging post holes for a wire fence round the new trees we had planted on Harris's Hill. The late Hugh Shortt, Curator of the Salisbury Museum, said it came from the tip of Cornwall where that particular type of rock uniquely occurred. It would have been traded with as a pre-Ecu currency on the route which ran west to east across England.

I picked up a number of worked flints on the ridge above the allotments, a sunny south-facing work place where it didn't take a wild imagination to see the little hairy men napping their flints to make scrapers, shavers and arrow heads for export to foreign parts like Salisbury.

In the early summer I used to take a few decent trout from the Nadder on a blue winged olive, or Greenwell's Glory, or in May the grey Wulf, which seemed to simulate the Mayfly near enough to deceive a Wiltshire trout.

The big barn at Church Farm made an ideal home for my collection of Victorian hand presses and wood letter. Some of these I had bought from Wales and Yorkshire where, until recently, every village printer had an old Albion or Columbian press dating back to the mid-nineteenth century. My 1828 Columbian Press by George Clymer was given to me as a retiring present by T & A Constable of Edinburgh. I bought another Columbian, two Albion presses, two Imperials and a unique toggle or 'elbow' press by Ritchie of Edinburgh; not dated but probably made before 1860.

I was given some full cases of type by Constables and wood letter by other printers in the Westminster Press Group. William Caxton would have been quite at home in my printing barn. The techniques were identical to those used in the fifteenth century except that I inked the formes with a composition roller. Rollers were not used for inking before the 1890s. Caxton's pressmen would have used an ink ball, like a large inverted mushroom, covered with leather with which to apply ink evenly to the type surface.

In addition to programmes for the local flower show and fun posters for neighbours' children offering huge rewards for the capture of highwaymen and bank robbers, I printed a few slim volumes over the imprint, Perdix Press.

The first book I printed was a collection of verses written by my brother, Albert. He wrote some beautiful sonnets addressed to his wife, Muriel, and their children, and also some very sharp-edged, satirical verses, attacking pomposity wherever he found it, particularly if it was in the Church or the Labour Party.

On Winston Churchill's 80th birthday, the House of Commons rose to its feet to acknowledge his entry; all except Michael Foot, who remained seated. Albert wrote:

CHURL

Acknowledging his stature and his fame
The whole house welcomed him with loud acclaim;
But Michael, scion of the Cornish Feet
Acknowledging his stature, kept his seat.

And of an Anglican bishop who had testified – during the trial of Penguin Books under the obscenity law following the first publication of *Lady Chatterley's Lover* – that the passage complained of had 'a sacramental quality', my brother wrote:

For a Prelate

The language of the closet door,
The morals of the hutch,
Despite the jury's verdict
Do not impress me much;
But the thought above all others
That sickens and appals
Is of consecrated Bishops
Talking sacramental balls.

And, by way of contrast, a Rondeau for Simon, his first son:

His solemn eyes that gently pour
Dark radiance from his soul's deep store,
Cast magic spells, and by their beams
Bend all our wills to his sole schemes
As old enchanters did of yore.

And when he laughs at antique lore
Of childhood's days, we laugh the more
And weep with him when tear-mist steams
    His solemn eyes.

Oh, when some maiden, stricken sore
As ne'er love wounded maid before
Shall see in them the thrilling themes
Of all her secret, singing dreams,
All Paradise she'll barter for
    His solemn eyes.

I set and proofed *13 Spells* for Jeni Cousyn in 1978 but it was never published. I took exception to the bitter words Jeni used to describe a childless woman. She said the attacking words were the means of exorcising the spell of barrenness.

I printed fifty copies of *Ten Poems* by Joan Barton in 1979 and sixty of *The Way of a Cook with a Trout* by Roger Monk who was then a chef at the Ritz in London.

After our move from Sutton Mandeville to Salisbury, there followed a dozen more titles of which an edition of *The Prologue to the Canterbury Tales* in 1985 was possibly the most important. The idea came from Mark Franklin, my literary counsellor, guide and friend, who wrote prefaces for several of my books. Mark, a graduate of Stanford and Oxford who had studied under Neville Coghill, the great Chaucerian authority, was a frequent visitor over the years. He taught literature and languages at a college in Dorset.

I obtained permission from Penguin Books, who held the copyright, to use the text of Coghill's modern translation of the *Canterbury Tales.* At first they asked for a reproduction fee which added up to more than £400. I wrote to Nick Whetton, the executive in charge of reproduction rights, and pointed out that the Owen Estate and Chatto and Windus had only charged £10 for the reproduction rights of Wilfred Owen's *War Poems* which I published in 1983. I said my edition would be limited to 200 copies, that I only wanted to use the *Prologue* not the entire works of Geoffrey Chaucer, and that a fee of £400 would price my slim volume out of the market. I then 'phoned Nick Whetton who turned out to be not only reasonable but interested, enthusiastic and generous.

'What would you consider to be a reasonable sum?' he asked.

'Well,' I hesitated in reply, 'I could recover, say, £40.'

'Right,' he said. 'Knock one of the noughts off my fee invoice and send me £40. We'll call that a deal.'

I hand-set the Prologue in 14 point Bembo type. Howard Phipps produced wood engravings of Chaucer for a frontispiece and the Knight on a prancing charger, with Wardour Castle in the background.

I planned the Coghill version to go on the left-hand, the verso, and an early Chaucerian text on the facing recto pages. I was going to print, from polymer plates, a facsimile of the matching pages from Robart Toye's edition, printed in St. Paul's Churchyard in c. 1545–48, a complete copy of which I had on the shelf. I showed a proof of one of these pages to Dr. Lotte Hellinga, a world authority on early books, and Deputy Director of the British Library. She asked why on earth I was using that unattractive type face: why not use the 1476 Caxton first edition which they had in the library? This unique volume, printed from a type described by Dr. Hellinga as '... inspired by the style of the luxurious Burgundian manuscripts ... adapted to an elegant typographical form ...' was made available, photographed and printed for me by photo-lithography.

When the book was published in September, 1985, it was very well reviewed and sold out within the year. I sold fifteen copies in Japan, fourteen in America and others in Holland, Switzerland, Canada and Ireland. The total cost of *The Prologue*, cash paid out, was £3,350 with no charge for the letterpress printing which I did myself; and the total revenue was £3,469, leaving a surplus of £119 for my planning, designing, typesetting and printing. Not to be recommended, as I told another aspiring private press printer, as a means of making a fortune, but, as young Michael Chater, the paper maker, told me when I was in a nerve-wracked state in Leeds in 1947: 'Very good for the soul.'

Tables manners for children or *Stans puer ad mensam* was another Perdix title which received praise from bibliophiles both in England and America. It was a facsimile reprint of John Lydgate's book of courtesy in the black letter type used by Caxton in his first edition dated 1476, accompanied on facing pages by Professor Nicholas Orme's modern translation and preceded by a scholarly foreword by Dr. Hellinga.

Dr. Hellinga had suggested that I take on this fifteenth century moral guide for young people, mainly because only one complete copy of the original Caxton edition survived and that was at the Huntington Library in San Marino, California. I wrote to the Huntington who not only gave permission to reproduce their unique Caxton, but provided, for the remarkably small fee of $115.00, 10 × 8 inch photographs of the black letter pages for me to use for the photo-litho facsimile pages.

I printed 265 copies on my 10 × 15 Arab platen and sold out in six months; 15 copies with vellum bindings at £85 and 250 copies in embossed cloth at £18. This time the margin for my own editing, setting and printing labours was £1200. I had evidently got the sums right, or less wrong, on this project.

In the private press business these experiences are about par for the course – you win some, you lose some – but essentially you please yourself. The economics of the game have to come second. Horace Walpole's Strawberry Hill Press must have been an aristocratic hobby; William Morris's Kelmscott Press was probably financed by his business activities in the arts and crafts movement. Today there are about 300 private presses in the U.K. of which a dozen are highly competent, well equipped establishments, producing the finest books to the highest standards – and providing a living for their talented owners.

The eccentrics are also there. Count Potocki of Montalk spends most of his time producing and publishing libel and slander against his sworn enemies, the Powys family. I met Potocki in Wimborne Minster when he asked me to help improve the impression on his rusty, aged platen press.

When I gaze out of the window of the room in which I am writing in The Close in Salisbury, I can see the

Cathedral Spire, with a crow's nest of scaffolding at the 375 ft level where the masons are replacing stones rotted by age and acid rain, so that the elegant structure will not totally collapse. Around the inner walls of our Tudor-ceilinged room are the two thousand books which have been collected over the years in about equal numbers by Betty and me. Betty has always been an avid reader and collector, particularly of children's books. I read very little as a child and was such a slow reader and restless character that I seldom sat down for long enough to finish a chapter. I could number on the fingers of one hand the books I read at school: *Last of the Mohicans*; *Around the World in Eighty Days*; *Just William* and part of *The Count of Monte Cristo*, the latter book so drearily printed in small type and grey ink that it was purgatory even to look at.

The first time I went to Harrogate Municipal Library, in about 1924, I asked the assistant if they had any books by Geoffrey Farnol. I was snubbed with a curt 'no' and left standing humiliated, feeling ashamed for having asked a silly question. I never went to a library again until I was sixty, when I got a reader's ticket for the British Library and benefitted immeasurably from the facilities the Library provided. In Salisbury, we are incredibly lucky to have a fine library with patient, helpful assistants who, to coin a phrase, serve above and beyond the call of duty.

Book collecting is an ancient and often eccentric occupation. In the 16th century, Archbishop Matthew Parker not only collected books from the disbanded monasteries, he also had agents all over Europe buying books which are now in the library at Corpus Christi College in Cambridge.

Why do people collect books? One famous bookman, John Carter, explains: 'Magpies have an acquisitive passion, and a similar passion afflicts one in a hundred of the human race.' Sir Thomas Phillips was a celebrated bibliomaniac (1792–1872). His declared intention was to get a copy of every book in the world. He bought 16,000 manuscripts in one year. His library sale by Sotheby's took more than 32 days, and on the 32nd day, there were still 500 lots.

In my late teens, I began to be hungry for books and for the ideas they contained. I read a wildly random selection of writers, largely prompted by my brother Albert's tastes. I read Shaw's prefaces but not the plays; some of Guy de Maupassant, Boccaccio, Schopenhauer and *War and Peace*, often without a clue as to the meaning of half the words and often reading a page two or three times over to get the gist of it, but always intrigued by the sound the words made in my head – like the little boy who said he liked sound radio better than television because the pictures were better. I really wanted someone to give me a reading list to follow and often asked, but never found the answer, which would have been, surely, the WEA or the Open University if it had existed at that time.

When I was sixty and had started to think of retiring, Betty began to worry about how I would occupy my time after leading a fairly busy life in newspaper production and printing management. She thought that books could provide a continuing interest for me; printing them, producing small editions of poetry, and collecting private press and early printed books. Betty was already established in collecting Victorian children's books, and rapidly becoming an authority on Beatrix Potter and

Meggendorfer, the early master of the art of moveable and pop-up books.

So one day, when Betty was bidding at a book sale at Hodgson's Rooms in Chancery Lane, London, I went along, too. I easily caught the infection or, as they would say in Yorkshire, 'got smittled' with a mild dose of bibliomania. I say a mild dose, because I became a regular buyer for several years but did not load the floors and staircase of my house as some have done, creating such a weight of unread books that the beams collapse and the stairs crumble.

Hodgson's Rooms had a fantastic atmosphere, a cross between a high court, a church and a market stall. Wilfred Hodgson conducted sales from the rostrum and after Sotheby's took over in 1967, Lord John Kerr was often in the chair. At the Clerk's desk was the inimitable Frank Snelling, with his phenomenal memory for names and faces, his eagle eye scanning the room for bids. His book, *Rare Books and Rarer People* (Werner Shaw, 1982) gives ample evidence of his skill in recalling the faces he had seen and describing the character behind the mask.

Leading book dealers of the day sat round the green baize table in front of the rostrum, always in their regular places. Eric Barton, who kept a bookshop on Richmond Hill, called them the merchant bankers. They could certainly put up a bid for a quarter of a million for a rare fifteenth century item or a medieval manuscript, by merely raising an eyebrow. I joined in the bidding, or sometimes asked a friendly dealer to assess the book and bid for me, for lots connected with the history of printing; not just books about books – although I did buy some of the standard works of reference by Dibdin and Percy Muir and, more recently, Ruari McLean – but mainly examples of what has happened in print since 1500. The incunabula, books printed before 1500 in the time of 'the cradle of printing', fetch prices well outside the budget of an ordinary collector of modest means.

My aim was to acquire good representative works, covering the fifteenth to the twentieth centuries, by distinguished printers, especially the scholar-printers like Aldus Manutius and the Estiennes, and type designer-printers like Baskerville, Bodoni, Morris and Mardersteig. Typical purchases, costing from £30 to £100, were a number of Aldine classics starting with a Martialis dated December 1501; a 1545 *Works of Geoffrey Chaucer* printed in St. Paul's Churchyard; a *Greek New Testament* printed by Robert Stephanus in Paris in 1549; *Cicero* by Elzevier of Leiden, 1630. The Chaucer was in tattered condition when I bought it but I had it restored beautifully by Bill Fairweather, a bookbinder who lived and worked on a narrow boat on the Thames at Kingston.

Many of these early printers were scholars first, publishers second and only printers as a means of getting books to a mass market. Some wrote commentaries on the scriptures which got them into deep trouble with the Vatican; they translated from Greek into Latin into vernacular Italian and French, and had Greek types cut to print pocket editions in the original language. I studied the lives of these great book makers to get the feel of their turbulent times.

A benchmark in English typography was established in the eighteenth century by John Baskerville of Birmingham whose exquisite prayer books and his *Paradise Lost* are on my shelves next to Bewick's *British Birds and Quadrupeds*, both fine examples of the wood engraver's art and not only distinguished for their natural history contents and fine illustrations but also for technical innovation: for example, the way Bewick developed the cutting of blocks on the end grain of boxwood so that their fine lines would stand up to the longer print runs then being demanded by the growing market for books.

Representing the 19th century, I have books from Whittingham's Chiswick Press; also a fine calf-gilt quarto of the *Poems and Letters* of Thomas Gray, amongst others, and from William Morris's Kelmscott Press in the 'nineties; the *Poems of John Keats* bound by the Guild of Women Binders, *Child Christopher* and *Love is Enough* in Limp vellum with the title page woodcut design by Burne-Jones. The great English private presses started in the 1890s and running into the 20th century, are represented by Kelmscott, Doves, Ashendene, Vale, Eragny, Essex House and the Gregynog Press in Wales.

Finally, central to the theme of this collection of distinguished scholar-printers, I have a number of the works of Giovanni Mardersteig – whom I met in London a few years ago – printed at his Officina Bodoni in Verona. Nothing less than a complete book could adequately describe this great man and his masterpieces of scholarship, design and printing. He was solidly in the tradition of Aldus Manutius in Venice and Robert Stephanus in Paris in the late 15th and early 16th centuries. He did his own research and translations, designed his own types, commissioned the paper-making and the illustrations, controlled the presswork and the binding, with the net result that his press, Officina Bodoni, produced what must rate as some of the finest books of this century. He died on December 27th, 1977, a great loss to the art of the book.

I read all the books I buy that are in English which

probably makes me unique among collectors. Many book collectors never seem to open their purchases for fear of finger-marking a page or causing a crack in the spine. Those books in Greek and Latin, I am just happy to gloat over and treat with affection.

No self-respecting collector needs to cook up a reason or excuse for collecting but he may sometimes need to justify spending more than he can really afford on a coveted title. I have known collectors buy a book for, say, £45 and ask the dealer for a copy invoice for £4.50 'to show her at home'. But it is a rewarding and recreative hobby.

My purchases now are limited to moderately priced volumes from the growing number of contemporary private presses. In the meantime, Betty has not been idle. She has a distinguished collection of 'Juveniles', as the trade calls children's books, and she is not infrequently referred to by dealers for an opinion as to the authenticity of a doubtful Beatrix Potter 'first'. Her Juveniles span the years from 1535 to 1990.

It is our way of life that in matters of hobbies, books, fishing, painting, even gardening, we each strictly mind our own business. I do press books, she does Juveniles. She grows flowers, I plant potatoes. Wherever we overlap or disagree, we compromise – I concede.

10

RESEARCH INTO EARLIEST PRINTING METHODS. LIFE IN THE CATHEDRAL CLOSE.

IN MARKED CONTRAST to my encounter at Harrogate library fifty years earlier, my first contact with the British Library in London was an adventure and a delight which set me off on a new tack – bibliographical research. The BL has its base in Great Russell Street, in the same building as the British Museum of which it was once part. I had been before to hear lectures by my good friend, John Dreyfus, and to see exhibitions on the works of Stanley Morison and Giovanni Mardersteig which were mounted by John Barr. On these occasions I had viewed the King's Library with awe, peeping into the great circular-domed Reading Room where Karl Marx did his homework when writing 'Das Kapital'. Now I was to be initiated and involved in the minor – but for me – challenging task of trying to solve problems about methods of printing in the mid-fifteenth century, in Gutenberg's town of Mainz.

From various sources, dealers and bookbinders, I had collected a number of single printed leaves from very early, pre-1500, printed books. Known as binders' or printers' waste, these single sheets have at some time been pasted together to make up boards for book covers, replacing the oak boards used earlier. With careful treatment these individual sheets can be separated out when they sometimes prove to be leaves from rare, even unrecorded works. One of my leaves came from a book printed at Subiaco near Rome in 1471 by Sweynheim and Pannartz, who left Germany and introduced the first printing press into Italy at the monastery of St. Scolastica, near Subiaco, then, three or four years later, in Rome. This folio sheet was printed on a heavy laid paper in a robust roman type which was to be re-drawn by Emery Walker in 1900 and re-cut by E.P. Prince for St. John Hornby to use at his Ashendene Press. I had other leaves or fragments (incomplete leaves) from books printed in Cologne in 1485, Venice in 1495 and Toledo in 1535.

I also had a number of unidentified leaves which I thought, after looking up references, seemed to resemble early printing from Spain but I could not be certain. So I took them to the British Library and asked John Barr to introduce me to someone in the Department of Rare Books, which was how I came to meet Dr. Lotte Hellinga. She received me warmly, and I showed her the prints that had puzzled me, asking her if they came from Spain.

'No,' she said, after a cursory look. 'That is Anton Koberger, Nuremberg, probably 1470s: that is his lower-case 'g'. The type probably came from Cologne.'

With this opinion, Dr. Hellinga reinforced something I had really known long before: the difference between a well-informed amateur in books and typography and a thorough-going professional. She went on to tell me that Koberger, famous for his printing of Schedel's *Nuremberg Chronicle* in 1493, had lived at No.3 Burgstrasse and his godson, Albrecht Dürer, at No. 27. They had collaborated closely on the *Chronicle* illustrations. My leaves of

Koberger's *Pantheologia* ran from folio 318 recto. The British Library, of course, has the complete work in two massive volumes.

That little problem being satisfactorily resolved, Dr.Hellinga then asked me, as a veteran practical printer, how I thought certain words in large type had come to be fitted into solid pages of a smaller type in a book she had open on her cluttered desk in the bowels of the Library. It was *Yearbook 35 Henry VI*, printed in 1481/2 by Lettou and Machlinia whose workshop was next to All Saints Church in the City. We agreed that they had not used Letraset!

I made a quick guess that the big letters had been filed to fit, and suggested that if I could be provided with a few Polaroid prints of the pages in question, I would simulate the effect with my own type and hand press at home and write a memorandum on the methods used. This I did, showing how the 'beards' of the larger letters, except where they supported descending characters, g, j, and q, were either filed off; or how the types, with these descending exceptions, had been cast on the same size body as the smaller types leaving the descenders, still on their larger bodies, to be accommodated by re-spacing the next line so that the descending parts of the letters fell between the words.

There is a bit more to this fairly simple technical question than appears at first glance. It had not been satisfactorily answered before although looked at by many bibliophiles. The type in question was identical with, or very closely related to, the third type used by Caxton and was probably made by his typefounder, Johann Veldener at Louvain. The alignment of the *Yearbook* characters was much less regular than those seen in

Caxton's printing, which made me think that Machlinia might have borrowed or hired the matrices from Veldener and, with much less skill, cast his own type: in which case he would have been the first typefounder in England. I wrote a paper giving an account of my experiments and opinions on this obscure little problem. It was illustrated and published in the *British Library Journal* (*A Use of Caxton's Type*, Vol. 9, No. 1, 1983).

Sponsored as a research student by Dr. Hellinga, I was now a card-carrying member of the Library, greatly enjoying the access this provided to its fabulous collection of rare books. In 1984, I came across a long article by Dr. Paul Needham of the Pierpont Morgan Library in New York, printed in the Papers of the Bibliographical Society of America (Vol. 67, 1982), in which he stated that the *Catholicon* of Johannes Balbus, printed (perhaps by Gutenberg press) in Mainz, was not printed from single types assembled into lines but from two-line slugs – sticks of type metal with two lines of characters cast in relief to create the printing surface. I was asked at the Library what I thought of this theory and the further point in Dr. Needham's thesis that the printing formes had been kept standing for twelve years to print editions in 1460, 1468 and 1472.

My immediate reply was 'Rubbish!'. Was it likely that the Mainz printer was going to hold maybe seven tons of costly type metal for twelve years against the possibility of a reprint? And who would go to the trouble and expense of casting slugs for the one book when a by now familiar practice was in regular use in Mainz, that of casting single characters, which could be used and re-used on other titles? Slug casting as a common means of production did not emerge for another four hundred years and stereotyping, which could have produced two-line stereos had this been even remotely practical for a massive seven hundred and forty-page folio book, appeared on the scene around 1690. But Dr. Needham's serious research which had been pursued in great depth, needed much more consideration than my off-the-cuff dismissal.

During 1984, I went up to the Library each month and spent a day poring over their three copies of the *Catholicon*: one printed on vellum, and the other two on different watermarked papers. I checked every page of all three issues for typographical idiosyncrasies, and found plenty. These I recorded in copious notes and the Library staff photographed and made slides for me of the more visual effects, using oblique lighting to throw up the blind emboss marks made by bearer quads and the type impressions in the paper. I also visited the Bodleian Library in Oxford to examine their *Catholicon* which was printed on a different paper from the two paper copies at the BL. Watermarks play a significant role in bibliographical forensics. (Dr. Needham arrived at his theory of a twelve-year gap in the dating of the *Catholicon* copies from the first dates when the papers used for them appeared with proven dates in other publications).

My thesis, if that is not too pompous a word to describe my first steps into bibliographical academia, took up sixteen pages of small print in the Spring number of *The Book Collector* (*Printing the Mainz Catholicon*, Spring, 1986). It might be summarized briefly as follows:

1. Two-line slugs could have been invented but this is unlikely, and even if they were, they would have been so

uneconomic that their use would have been discontinued long before completion of the Catholicon first issue.

2. It is more likely that the three issues were printed concurrently on three presses in the same pressroom so that the total print run covering the vellum copies and the differently watermarked makings of paper could be equitably shared between three publishers or independent backers, each with his own pressman and paper, the whole project being too large to be financed by any one of them.

3. The irregular indentation of pairs of lines in random positions, which caused Dr. Needham to conclude that two-line slugs had been used, was caused very simply by the line-end spaces and bearer quads varying in width.

When *The Book Collector* article appeared, naturally enough, Dr. Needham was not amused. What was uncalled for, though, was the way he berated Dr. Hellinga and *The Book Collector* editor, Nicolas Barker, for prompting my investigation and encouraging me in it with the apparent intention of discrediting his own work. This could not have been further from the truth.

In December 1985, I was invited to present my paper to an 'Arbeitsgespräch', or colloquium, which was being held solely on the printing of the *Catholicon* at the Herzog August Bibliothek in Wolfenbüttel near Hanover in Germany. At first I declined, partly on account of the language problem, having only a little tourist German, and partly because I was not anxious to dive into this controversial and highly academic maelstrom any deeper than I had done with the technical paper already published. The list of participants looked quite formidable: twenty professors and Herr Doktors, a few librarians and two students.

Finally, I was persuaded by Dr. Martin Boghardt, the organiser, to attend and give my paper in English, as a printer's view on an early printing problem. There would be seven other papers, including contributions by Dr. Hellinga, Dr. Needham and other authorities on mid-fifteenth century printing in Mainz, notable amongst whom was Professor (Baron) Dr. Wolfgang von Stromer Freiherr von Reichenbach, whose forebears were the first paper makers in Germany.

At dinner, the large and most amiable Baron, aware of my lack of German, took me in hand as his personal guest and told me about his family. They were not only the first paper makers in Germany but also the first wire drawers, a trade in which they held a monopoly until they diversified into gun barrels. As a younger man, he had been an astro-physicist, but when all his brothers were killed in the Second World War, he had to turn to directing the family businesses; hence his expertise in paper technology and history. On arrival at the seminar reception, I had heard the secretary chide the Baron for not having replied to a letter about accommodation.

'I am very sorry,' he said, 'But I have been too busy re-roofing the castle.'

My turn to speak came on the second morning. The procedure was formal: applause after each paper was brief and restrained, consisting of gently tapping the table with the knuckle of one index finger. I spoke for about forty minutes and showed a few slides. It would have been better if I had cut the talk by half and stuck more closely to the central theme. However, I received courteous applause and appreciative glances from several members of the learned audience. Questions followed. Dr. Needham was not slow with some gratuitous sarcasm to the effect that my paper had little resemblance to genuine research and was no more than a long and rhetorical account of how Mr. Partridge thought printers might have worked in Mainz in the fifteenth century.

My paper was generally acknowledged as a useful, thought-provoking contribution to the long-running and still unresolved questions of what precise methods were used in printing of the *Catholicon*; when it was printed and by whom? Like the mystery of the Turin Shroud, the problem of the *Catholicon* refuses to go away. It has been studied for a century. Nor will it be resolved until more hard evidence turns up.

Carbon dating seems to have placed the origins of the Shroud in the Middle Ages but this is still being disputed. Dating the *Catholicon* is proving more difficult despite words in the colophon saying that all copies were printed in the '1460s'.

* * *

By a combination of guile and good fortune, I managed to retire gradually, running down what had been a fully active business life, and progressively building up less demanding occupations and things done just for fun. Our house in Sutton Mandeville proved to be such an ideal place to do this that I felt I could have run courses on 'How to Retire Successfully'. Both Betty and I were busy all day doing things we loved to do, which sometimes involved just leaning on the gate and watching cloud shadows on the hillside across the valley. Betty was painting, embroidering, cooking and creating a garden; while I was clearing and re-planting parts of the wood, sawing up logs for the huge open fires, digging the vegetable plot and printing poetry books.

I called the modest printing and publishing venture after Perdix the craftsman, nephew of Daedalus and cousin of Icarus. Daedalus became jealous of the extraordinary skills shown by Perdix and threw him off the Acropolis. And as Robert Graves tells in his *Greek Myths*, Zeus turned the boy into a partridge so that he should not crash to the ground. Because Icarus had been killed by flying too near to the sun, Perdix only flew low, as the wily partridge does today, seldom rising above hedge top level.

On summer evenings, I fished for trout at Spencer's Mill on the Nadder and, in time, was elected to the Parish Council. I still had one or two consultancy retainers in London which gave me an excuse to go up there from time to time, to earn fees and wine and dine with old Fleet Street cronies. I avoided taking up golf again as I was never very good at the game and could only get worse.

I should have guessed that this idyllic life with which we were blessed for ten years was too good to be true. Betty went to the doctor one day for a check on something that had been worrying her for a while and came back with the news that she must go into hospital immediately for a cancer operation. Her inner anxieties were not apparent. 'What must be, must be,' she said, showing no more alarm than if she was going for a tooth extraction instead of a quick hysterectomy. Such is the courage of women – as exemplified by my wife. It may have been this brave, resourceful attitude that contributed to her total recovery to robust health within three months.

When Betty came home from hospital, we did a lot of thinking and decided it might be wise to move from Church Farm, which was quite remote, and find a house in Salisbury: two bedrooms, large kitchen, small garden and a workshop, and not more than five minutes walk from Marks & Spencer! We had moved house six times since our marriage and each time the 'job specification' was written on the back of a postcard in these essential terms, depending on our growing (or diminishing) family and the place where I was to earn my living. We always planned well ahead of the need to move and were usually lucky in finding the right place.

How could we follow the charm and beauty of Church Farm and still have a nice house with small garden and workshop in the middle of Salisbury? We looked at several prospects, including an empty, run down medieval house – 21, The Close – which had mushrooms growing through the wet, flagged floor and ivy on the inside and outside walls. It was not on the market but some restoration work was going on with the stone-mullioned windows. Climbing over scaffolding and rubble, we looked through the back windows and Betty said, 'What marvellously proportioned rooms, and look, here's a cellar that would make you a press room.' It was, in fact, a private chapel of thirteenth-century origin.

We went to see the estate agent who told us that there was little chance of us getting the place because the Dean and Chapter could not decide what to do with it. Over the next year, we looked at other possibilities and either turned them down or were gazumped. One day, the agent rang and informed me that the Dean and Chapter were meeting to decide on and approve a plan for restoring No. 21 and putting it on the market; as we were first on his list, he would tell us the score if we went in the next day. So in we went.

The house was to be divided into one ground floor and two upstairs flats. An architect's plans had been approved and a developer had been licensed to carry out the work and dispose of the three flats. A sixty-year lease was being offered and the price for the ground floor flat was £125,000, subject to a small ground rent and maintenance charge. We already had an offer in excess of this sum for Church Farm so it took Betty and me about thirty seconds to arrive at a unanimous decision and go ahead with the purchase.

I asked the agent what would happen next, and if we were in for a silent auction. 'No,' he replied, 'You say yes, you pay a deposit. I draw a line across the book, and the property is yours. Couldn't be simpler.'

To avoid having to go to the bank for a bridging loan, we organised completing the sale of Church Farm and the purchase of the lease on No.21 at the same time – twelve noon on November 15th, 1983, so that we could be settled in for Christmas.

During the preceding months, the building and restoration work had been carried out, by and large satisfactorily but with one or two black marks. On the instructions of the developer, who had better be nameless, a unique eighteenth-century lantern window was removed for his personal use. He did offer to return it at a price, but when pressed said that he no longer had it. It was a large, half lantern-shaped extension to a window over-looking the yard, which could be opened from the room to allow a lit candle or oil lamp to be placed to shine over the yard. It has been described as a rare 'hospitality window'.

I took up the matter with the house agent, the Chapter Clerk and finally, the District Council who all agreed that the removal of this feature on a listed building was a scandal, but when the developer dug in his heels and there was a question of legal action, they all feebly gave up. The developer's case rested on the fact that the lantern was not specifically detailed on the restoration plans.

The other disaster area was the plumbing: trouble caused by careless, incompetent work and lack of supervision. The hot and cold water pipes are laid together and embedded in concrete, with the result that we get three gallons of tepid water out of the cold tap and three gallons of cold water from the hot tap before we get anything remotely like H & C. Even the hose pipe tap in the yard gives water warmed by indirect heat. Then we had two copper pipe joints which were put together but not soldered. One was in an upstairs bathroom so that as soon as the water was turned on, a flood came through our larder ceiling: the other was a central heating pipe joint, also never soldered, which we eventually located under the concrete diningroom floor. This 'joint' must have blown as soon as it was fitted and been leaking furiously; for two years I was disturbed by the constant flow into the header tank. We had an invasion of plumbers, heating engineers and Water Board officials trying to locate this, by now, massive leak. When it was found, after the diningroom floor had been dug up with a pneumatic drill, it was quickly mended, but not before many thousands of gallons of water had flowed into the foundations. Fortunately, we are on well-drained gravel so no permanent damage was done.

The central heating boiler cracked as soon as it was lit but had been replaced before we came on the scene. Finally, and craziest of all, the upstairs water pipes had been left unlagged and were exposed to the cold air blowing in through ventilation grills and gaps in the masonry in 1986, when the temperature fell to ten below zero. The pipes burst and a minor Niagara poured through our kitchen ceiling. The plumbers came quickly and mended the bursts while we and our neighbours bailed and mopped to stop the flood water flowing through the house. But wait! On the next night, the pipes burst again and the deluge was dealt with as before. The plumber had repaired the pipes well enough but had forgotten to lag them or close up the ventilation holes. Apart from these minor disruptions, we are very happy with what is now a warm, dry and spacious super-flat.

'Aula le Stage', as No. 21 The Close is called, was first occupied in 1250c. It was built as a residence for one of the Canons after the main building of the Cathedral was completed but before the Tower and Spire were added. The distinctive name describes a house with an upper chamber or first floor, which would have been unusual at that early date. C.R. Everett described it in the *Wiltshire Archaeological Magazine* (Vol. 149, 1941) as 'one of the largest and most important of the canonical houses.'

Tourists often stop to photograph and admire the house and the garden Betty has created from heaps of builders' rubble: we sometimes invite them to see inside with the little private chapel at the back. I derive a childish pleasure from their reactions when I tell them that the new part is Tudor. The original chapel was where the kitchen now stands. In 1464, the Cathedral was polluted by a 'great effusion of blood' caused by a fight between William Powell, altarist, and Robert

Bellrynger. The Cathedral was closed until the Bishop could be brought back from Sherborne where he had been staying, to reconsecrate the building. During this period of closure, the chapel at 'Aula le Stage' was used for the celebration of divine service. It was also used by the clergy to hold the Chapter meetings when the Chapter House was too cold.

Effusions of blood seem to have been a popular way of settling disputes in those days. In 1449, a divorce case was being heard in the Bishop's Consistory Court when the wife in question declared that her husband was a hermaphrodite; whereupon 'the husband nearly killed the woman' in the Cathedral near the place where the Court was sitting and 'caused a great effusion of blood.'

'Aula le Stage' is not haunted by humans although reading its recorded history makes one think that it well might have been; but it is not without supernatural manifestations. If you dig a trench more than a spade deep in the garden or the driveway and listen carefully, you can hear the hooves of long-dead horses stamping on the gravel as they wait for the coachman's order to move.

When the house ceased to be a canonry on the death of Canon Bowles in 1850, the chapel was converted into a kitchen and the beer cellar was turned into an oratory. Whether the lay occupants took away all the beer barrels, we cannot be certain, but it is recorded that Canon William Lisle Bowles left seventy-two dozen bottles of port in the wine cellar. The bibulous canon wrote sonnets and edited a ten-volume edition of the works of Alexander Pope.

Under its more recent lay occupants, the oratory has been an air raid shelter, a student's room, and now it houses my three hand-presses, type and hand-made paper. The lease prohibits the use of any part of the house for anything other than a private residential purpose, so when I was about to start my small publishing activities, I invited Dean Sydney Evans to come and see what I was up to. He looked at the Canterbury Tales prologue that I had in proofs and at the type pages on the stone and said, after the manner of Lord Nelson, 'I see no commercial activity. We'll call it the Chapel of the Words.'

I had a similar enlightened reaction from the Inland Revenue inspector when I reported that I intended to sell an occasional edition of a hundred poetry books. 'Can't see you making a taxable profit that way,' he said. 'If you start submitting returns, I can see that we should be paying you. So while it is at this scale, let's call it a hobby.'

In printing trades union terms – and I still hold a card in the National Graphical Association – I have now become the father of my own chapel. Being my own father, I must be a biological sport or a genetic first issue.

* * *

Reflections

Salisbury Cathedral Close is the friendliest village we have ever lived in. On the day of our arrival with the furniture van, our next door neighbour, Mrs. Shemilt, turned up at the front door with a huge, piping hot quiche and a broad smile. 'Meals on wheels,' she announced, and disappeared before I could say thank you. What a lovely welcome; in our experience, quite typical of the people in The Close today. It was not always like this. We had been warned that it would be cliquey but things have changed for the better since Anthony Trollope's day, and probably most markedly in the years since the Second World War.

Dissent in one form or another has been in my blood and my upbringing so it is not surprising that my approach to the Church of England has always been touched with ambivalence. I have referred earlier to our Methodist connection in Harrogate; when our children were growing up in Leeds, I joined the Congregational Church, now the United Reformed, and served for several years as a deacon. Most of the years between childhood and maturity were spent in a limbo of religious doubt which still persists, even now that I am a practising Anglican and have been a member of the Cathedral Council.

Soon after we came here, I was attending the ten o'clock Eucharist with Betty; Canon Dudley Hodges came up to me afterwards and said, 'I was glad to see you at Communion, but I don't see your name on the Electoral Roll of members of the congregation. Betty is on but not you.'

'No,' I replied, 'I have never been confirmed into the Church.'

'You know what you are like,' he said, with a wry smile, 'You're like the chap who goes to the golf club and pays a green fee but never offers to join the club. It's time you became a member.'

I was not unwilling and the conversation turned from an invitation to a discussion of means and ends.

'We'll ask your neighbour, John O'Hara,' Dudley continued, 'if he will join with you. We'll meet at each other's houses for eight confirmation classes and I will see if Bishop Pike will confirm you in the Morning Chapel one weekday.' (Victor Pike, retired Chaplain General to HM Forces and former Bishop of Sherborne, lived in The Close).

We had classes with tea and cakes as Dudley took us through church history: from the first disciples, the Greek and Roman periods, the Greek Orthodox division, Martin Luther and the Reformation. He explained the significance of liturgy and ritual and finally briefed us on the form and content of the Eucharist and Confirmation services. There was a good deal of questioning and some friendly argument before the Canon, who is no mean advocate, said that he would talk to the Dean about arranging the service.

The Dean was not keen on our having a private little service in a side chapel; a bit hole-in-the-corner, he thought: 'Better go and have a word with the Bishop.' (John Baker).

Dudley saw the Bishop who said without hesitation: 'I would be very pleased to confirm your two mature candidates in my own chapel here in the house. Tell them to bring their families and friends and come on Wednesday at ten o'clock.'

So that is how I was received into the Anglican Church by John Sarum on January 16th, 1985, in my seventy-fourth year. It was a most moving service with the Bishop fully robed and mitred, after which we adjourned for coffee and chat.

What does it feel like, you may well ask, to have become at this late stage a full-blown member of the Church? Well, there have been no great shafts of light from heaven or flashes of insight into the eternal mysteries of the spirit. I am still deeply conditioned by the nonconformist tradition and find the liturgy and ceremonial of the Cathedral, although full of grace and beauty and theatre, not essential to my efforts to follow the teachings of Christ. Sometimes I have been inclined to go along with Ignazio Silone, an Italian socialist, who wrote, in anticipation of his death: 'It seems to me that in the course of centuries a theological and liturgical elaboration has been superimposed over the essential Christian truths so as to make these unrecognisable.' (*A Need to Testify*. Iris Origo. Murray, 1984)

What I like best about the Cathedral services is the preaching, the standard of which is always good and often brilliant as the Dean and the three canons – Precentor, Chancellor and Treasurer – bring their scholarship and various skills to the pulpit. Best of all is the very definite feeling of having been made a member of a large, extended family of friends.

I have called this final, short chapter 'Reflections' rather than 'Conclusions' because although my first thoughts are often suspect, my second thoughts, after reflection, have usually proved to be fairly reliable. Indeed, I have earned my living over recent years as a consultant in the complicated business of printing by being able to examine problems and, after reflection, to come up with workable solutions.

I doubt if there has been another century in history when the world has had to face problems of change more acute than those of the period between the coronation of George V, when I was born, and this year of grace, 1991. Motoring, flying and radio were in their infancy when I was a boy; transistors, television and computers had not been invented. Splitting the atom, precursor to nuclear power and the Bomb, was a research project that the world might have been better off without. On the human side, I think we are a more compassionate nation than were the Victorians. Politics aside, there is now more concern for orphans and the elderly. Headingley Orphan Homes in the 1890s was completely filled with foundlings abandoned behind Leeds market or left on the orphanage doorstep by 'unfortunate' girls who had been thrown out of the house by angry parents. Bob Geldof's Band Aid appeal gave proof of the great store of goodwill and generosity that exists today in most unexpected quarters, and which can be tapped to help distressed peoples across the world: not only our own kith and kin but complete strangers whom we have never met.

On the other side of the coin, the crime rate has risen worldwide, producing new heights of terror. And since 1945, there have been more than a hundred and fifty separate wars around the world.

David North, who edited the *UK Press Gazette* when I was in Fleet Street, paid me the compliment of saying that I was always good at two thousand words. I have tried in these pages to put together a series of impressions of about that length as a personal record of encounters and experiences in this changing world.

Betty and I have been blessed with good fortune – safely coming through a war, solvent in business, sound in health after successful treatment, and with four grown-up children, all following their chosen careers, and three grandchildren. We have enjoyed long and happy lives still filled with a mutual love which continues to astonish us with its completeness and fulfilment.

Bibliography of

PERDIX PRESS
21 The Close
Salisbury, Wiltshire SP1 2EB

Verses. Written between 1935 and 1960 by the printer's brother, Albert Partridge. 25pp. 10 × 6⅝ inches. 16 point Bembo. 50 numbered copies printed black on Abbey Mills Pure White Text paper on a Columbian hand-press. 10 copies bound by Harry Bailey in Quarter morocco, lettered gold on spine, with marbled paper boards; 40 copies sewn and glued into green paper covers, cut flush, printed in black on front and spine. The first book from the press. Sutton Mandeville, *1977.*

13 Spells by Jeni Couzin. 1978. 66pp. 8¾ × 5 inches board set Bembo on 1858 Columbian hand-press. 16pp sewn into white cover. Only 12 copies printed. (6 for J.C. and 6 for W.P.) Not published due to printer's objection to words used to describe a childless woman. An altogether unhappy exercise.

Ten Poems by Joan Barton, bookseller of Salisbury, written between 1973 and 1978. 50 copies signed by poet and printer. Printed on a Columbian press. 20 pages, 9¾ × 6 inches. *1979.*

The Way of a Cook With a Trout by Roger Monk. Recipes for cooking and smoking trout and grayling. Sewn and glued in old gold cover paper with repro of 1486 woodcut of a fisherman from the 'Treatyse' on the cover. 24pp. $8\frac{3}{4} \times 5\frac{3}{4}$ inches. 60 signed copies. *1979.*

Three Little Ghostesses. Child's guide to food and drink in verses taken from the Oxford Nursery Rhyme Book. 100 copies for the Society of Private Printers. Hand set in Bembo, printed on an Imperial and an Albion press. Printed paper cover. Hand-made paper. $4\frac{3}{4} \times 2\frac{1}{2}$ inches. *1979.*

Start Reading Music by Michael Venner. A basic guide to the musical score. 20pp. $8\frac{1}{2} \times 5\frac{1}{2}$ inches. Sewn into printed Japanese vellum paper cover. Signed by author and printer. *1979.*

A Song for Rainmakers. Serbian Folk-Song translated by John Adlard. 10pp. $8\frac{1}{2} \times 5\frac{1}{4}$ inches. Abbey Mills paper sewn into green printed cover paper. *June 1980.* 50 copies signed by the author.

Selected Poems by William Barnes. Selected and edited by Walter Partridge with a preface by Mark Franklin. Hand set, two wood engravings, limited to 100 signed and numbered copies. 34pp. 265 × 155mm. *June 1981.*

A (very) Concise History of Printing in Europe by Walter Partridge. A Chapbook produced for the Society of Private Printers. 200 copies printed. Text set in Linotype Baskerville. 6.2 × 3.8 inches. 16pp. Antique laid paper. 5 illustrations including 2 Bewick repros. Sutton Mandeville, 1982. Reset and reprinted four times. *1985, '86, '86, '91.*

The Nature Poetry of John Clare, selected and with an introduction by Mark Franklin. Hand set in Bembo type and printed on a hand-press (Arab and Albion), limited to 110 copies. 56pp. 265 × 160mm. Ten copies on Milbourne hand-made paper. 10 bound full water bison calf include signed original aquatint portrait of Clare by Norman Ackroyd. All copies numbered and signed. Sutton Mandeville, *1982.*

On White Horse Hill and other poems by Gilbert Waugh. 50 copies. 220 × 170mm. Hand set in Bembo type. Printed on an Arab platen on book wove. 18pp. Thread sewn and glued into limp card covers, cream and pale blue. Printed on front with title in flower border. Sutton Mandeville, *May 1983.*

War Poems by Wilfred Owen with a critical appraisal of Owen's work by Mark Franklin and five lino cut illustrations by Peter Paul Piech. Printed on an Arab platen. Set in Bembo, intro by hand, poems by Mouldtype monotype. 55pp on Basingwerk parchment, 265 × 160mm, limited to 110 copies signed by Franklin and the printer. Ten copies full calf; fifty full cloth; Winstanley binder; 50 limp Jap vellum, sewn and drawn on by W.P. Sutton Mandeville, *September 1983.*

First publication after the move to 21 The Close, Salisbury:

The Prologue to The Canterbury Tales by Geoffrey Chaucer in the original text from Caxton's 1476 first edition with a modern translation by Neville Coghill on facing pages. The Caxton black letter pages are photo litho facsimiles from the British Library copy printed by White Dove Press, Essex. 82pp. 260 × 180mm. Modern translation set in 14 pt. Bembo and printed on an Arab platen. 200 signed and numbered copies in full cloth. Ten copies numbered 1 to 10 in full calf with slip cases. *October 1984.*

'A letter to Emiko' by John Adlard. 100 copies, 4pp and cover hand set in Bembo, *1984.*

A letter from Lewis Chaucer by John Gohorry, in which

Gohorry narrates a dream undergone by ten year-old Lewis, son of Geoffrey Chaucer. The 'Letter is from the boy to his father'. 24pp. 250 × 165mm. Hand set in 14 pt. Bembo. Includes a small original wood engraving of the astrolabe and a lino cut of the dream by Howard Phipps. 100 copies signed by the poet. Thread sewn, drawn on printed limp cover £2.00 (Underpriced, sold out in ten days). Salisbury: *March 1985.*

Twelve Poems by Christopher Driver. 150 copies. 24pp. 230 × 150mm. Hand set. 14 pt. Bembo. Limp covers. *May 1985.*

Six Love Poems translated by John Adlard. 100 copies. 16pp. 8½ × 6 inches. Limp cover. Hand set in Bembo. *March 1986.*

Aula le Stage by Walter Partridge. A short history of a house of medieval origin in The Close at Sarum (No. 21, home of the Perdix Press). 16pp plus cover, 7¼ × 5¼ inches on Zerkall mould-made paper. *1987.*

Izaak Walton's *Life of George Herbert* with intro. by Canon Patrick Magee. Reprinted from an issue by SPCK printed in 1853 by Richard Clay, Bread St.Hill, London. 210 copies, various finishes, full morocco, quarter vellum and full cloth. *1987/8.*

8 Catalan Poems by Marià Mament. Translated by John Adlard. 16pp and cover 8½ × 6¼ inches. 100 copies. *1988.*

Table Manners for Children: Stans Puer Ad Mensam. A book of courtesy, written c.1400 by John Lydgate, first printed by Caxton, 1476. Translation and intro. by Professor Orme. Foreword by Dr. Lotte Hellinga. 41pp. 8¼ × 5½ inches. 265 copies on Lana Royal Crown mould-made paper. 250 in buckram boards and 15 full limp vellum. *1989.*

Homage to Franco Sacchetti. c.1400. Poems by Franco Sacchetti translated by John Adlard. 9 × 5¾ inches. 24pp and cover. Poems and stories. 150 copies. *1990.*

Journeyman by Walter Partridge. A printer's impressions through eighty years in a rapidly changing world. Computer set by Leaper & Gard Ltd, Bristol; printed by Antony Rowe, Chippenham. 500 copies. 8½ × 5½ inches. 176 pages. Buckram boards. *1991.*

All these Perdix Press titles, except Journeyman, 1991, are now out of print.

W.J.P./1991.